Books should be returned on or before the
last date stamped below.

23. SEP 99
28 OCT 1999
01 DEC 1999
23 FEB 2000
19 JUL 2000
-2 OCT 2000
-1 NOV 2000
30 NOV 2000
30 JAN 2001
-8 MAR 2001
18 JUN 2001
06 AUG 2001
21 AUG 2001
08 OCT 2001

11 FEB 2002
14 MAR 2002
11 APR 2002
30 MAY 2002
-7 AUG 2002
-2 OCT 2002

11 FEB 2003
19 APR 2003
-1 AUG 2003
27 AUG 2003
23 SEP 2003
17 DEC 2003

ABERDEENSHIRE
LIBRARY &
INFORMATION SERVICES
29 MAR 2008
WITHDRAWN
FROM LIBRARY

NORTH EAST of SCOTLAND LIBRARY SERVICE
MELDRUM MEG WAY, OLDMELDRUM

Roots in a northern
landscape : celebrations
of childhood in the

ABERDEENSHIRE
LIBRARY &
INFORMATION SERVICES
WITHDRAWN
FROM LIBRARY

X6

1081481

D0264867

Roots in a Northern Landscape

Celebrations of Childhood in the North East of Scotland

edited by

W Gordon Lawrence

ABERDEENSHIRE
LIBRARY &
INFORMATION SERVICES

WITHDRAWN
FROM LIBRARY

SCOTTISH CULTURAL PRESS
EDINBURGH

First published 1996
Scottish Cultural Press
Unit 14, Leith Walk Business Centre,
130 Leith Walk, Edinburgh EH6 5DT
Tel: 0131 555 5950 • Fax: 0131 555 5018

This selection copyright © 1996 Scottish Cultural Press
on behalf of the contributors

All rights reserved. No part of this publication may be reproduced, stored in a retrieval system, or transmitted in any form or by any means, electronic, mechanical, photocopying, recording or otherwise without the prior permission of Scottish Cultural Press

X6
10814481

British Library Cataloguing in Publication Data
A catalogue record for this book is available
from the British Library

ISBN: 1 898218 79 X

Printed and bound by
Cromwell Press, Melksham, Wiltshire

Contents

Acknowledgements

The publisher acknowledges with thanks permission to include the following in this volume:

W Gordon Lawrence

'Gi'e me the een again', reproduced with kind permission of the Aberdeen University Alumnus Association, from *Aberdeen University Review XLIX*: 1 (165) 1981.

Raymond Vettese

Reproduced with kind permission of the Saltire Society:

From *The Richt Noise and ither poems*, Macdonald Publishers, Edinburgh 1988 (Lines Review Editions), for which Raymond Vettese was awarded the Saltire Society's 'Scottish First Book Award' in 1988.

'Crystal Dancer' (extract), 'Words', 'A Window Life', 'The Horn, Yirdit' (extract), 'Tak Pooer' (extract), 'The Vieve Cry'.

From *A Keen New Air*, Saltire Society, Edinburgh 1995:

'This Antrin Day', 'Kist', 'The Barman's Tale', 'Willie's Tree', 'A Keen New Air' (extract), 'Shrunkelt'.

Roots in a Northern Landscape

All of us who have contributed to this collection of childhood memories were raised in the North East of Scotland. We write about our social world of fifty to sixty years ago which has substantially disappeared but continues to have a vivid reality in our memories and imagination. We each write of the particular spirit of place and time which we carry in our psyche no matter where we may be located now. Stuart Hood, for example, could readily evoke the geography of Montrose when he was with the Partisans in Italy during the war trying to find his way across the country.

Most of us were brought up speaking the two languages of Doric and English. Doric, I have found as an adult, has been my secret language. Because I have little opportunity to speak it I find it is the language of silent commentary behind the chosen words of courteous discourse. An ambitious, narcissistic colleague is a 'vratch' in my secret lexicon; a loved grandson a 'nickum'; sometimes I feel 'sair trachled' when trying to 'jalouse' the contents of a 'sotter' of books and papers; and when tired after a run of writing research reports and the like I have an image of myself 'rowin' barras o' neeps tae the nowt'. David Kerr Cameron and Raymond Vettese have probably stayed more than the rest of us with the language through which realities were conveyed to them as children, Raymond as a poet and David as someone who has written of the way of life of the North East crofter in a classic series of books. Cathie Imlah has never moved from the North East and Doric is what she often uses when reporting the results of her genealogical research, for example, which gives them nuances of meaning that would not be possible in English.

The Word for all of us was our beginning because it has been the basis of our adult livelihoods whether as novelists and poets or writing books and articles or as researchers and academics or film makers. The Word was instilled in the schools of the North East we attended. Marion (Cowie) Swogger was captivated by Shakespeare as a child even though it was through a somewhat louche teacher that she entered the world of drama. Most of us make reference to some of the teachers or dominies who taught us as children. I suspect everyone carries a private pantheon of those who taught them. I certainly am forever grateful that I was taught at Ferryhill Public School by Miss Hilda Clark between the ages of ten and twelve (1944–46). Every Friday morning we wrote our essay which would be marked over the weekend. The week before was spent in inwardly rehearsing it. A new word would be hoarded for possible use in the essay, a telling phrase cherished, the idea for a story sought. Books and the wireless were our sources of inspiration. As children we read and read in those days before the arrival of television. Miss Clark died in 1985 but occasionally I have the fantasy that one day I will write something that she will really like and praise, and award me three gold stars, and that she will break her rule of only giving nineteen out of twenty even for the best of work and give me the full score!

The subject of this collection is childhood, with the leitmotivs of landscape, education, and the loss of innocence running through each contribution. We have, furthermore, each tried to convey our understanding of the culture in which we were reared. To be sure, the look of distance lends enchantment. On that solid base of North East culture we may have cultivated subsequently sophistication and scholarship but, nevertheless, it always remains constant, ready to revisit us in dreams or when we meet someone who shares the same roots. It was a culture that rewarded couthiness and derided pretentiousness of any kind. We were brought up with the reminder that no matter how successful a person might be in the world there would always be someone to murmur, 'I kent his faither,' even beyond the grave.

A number of us were brought up in the country and would have had relations who crofted or farmed or were cottared and were visited for holidays. This grounded us in the rural reality of Buchan and the Mearns. And that rootedness in the dubs and the sharn has stayed with us but so has much else which came from the inherited North East respect for the mind that has enabled us to make our ways in the world. David Hay has spent much of his adult life puzzling out the meaning and significance of religious experience. Iain Davidson has given much of his professional life to educational psychology and the needs of blind and other disadvantaged children. I have been involved for the last thirty years in using psychoanalysis as a tool of cultural enquiry to understand conscious and unconscious life in groups and institutions. Each of us, in some measure, can claim to have been a loon or quine o' pairts and so each of us able to celebrate his or her childhood, acknowledging both its good and bad experiences. If we can give to you at least an inkling of what it was to be a child fifty years or so ago in the North East of Scotland we shall be pleased that you can share our gratitude.

W Gordon Lawrence
London
September 1996

THE COTTAR'S BAIRN

David Kerr Cameron

The old croft lay down from the road; she was sour ground and had soured the lives of the folk who had worked her. One fine afternoon in the early springtime an old man ran from her to one of the adjoining brae set parks of the neighbouring farmtoun where a horseman was striding out behind the chain harrows in the drouthy onset of seedtime. He 'hallo'd' him with frantic gestures of haste. 'Better be on yer bike, chiel,' the old man gasped. 'She's come tae her time!' Leaving horse and harrows where they stood the young ploughman bolted for his bicycle and pedalled, pursued by a thousand furies, to bring the doctor... I came into the world in the bed in the croft's ben end a few hours later and even now, these long years after, I cannot pass the site of my grandfather's house without a pang of pride and a sense, still, of belonging there, in that bare countryside 'lying quiet with farms'.

NOTHING, I believe, could better have fitted me for life than those joyous days of freedom around the Thirties farmtouns of my childhood. They seem to me now to have been idyllic; the seasons turning, unremitting in their cycle, and men turning with them. The world had a fine immutability then; for the cottar's bairn, nature and all that he saw in the parks around him imprinted an identity he never saw need to question. Or so it seems. They say that the old ploughmen of that northern countryside, as the years encroached and made them less able, cultivated the trick of tilting the sole of the plough in the furrow to make the task easier on themselves and on their Clydesdale pairs and it may well be that the bairn, with the endrig now in closer view, sees a scene softened by sentiment and distance – even distorted by exile. Yet I cannot think it is so, and he would be a poor ploughman who did not pause to cast his gaze on the furrow behind him...

When I look back it is on a dear bleak landscape that instilled a fine caution in the affairs of life; that imbued a dour resilience to ill fortune and a deep and stoic acceptance of things as they were. None of these qualities is inconsequential and, like so many more, I believe most fervently that I have been a beneficiary of the spirit and indomitable will of those folk of the old farmtouns, the only legacy they had to pass down in their generations, along with their sometimes unruly blood. (The remembrance now is of a folk with a broad, slow burning humour that was allusive rather than direct; that called no one a liar which would have been contentious, perhaps dangerous. Disbelief when it was called for could be slyly registered without confrontation with a serious shake of the head and a profound: 'D'ye tell me that noo?') I have felt myself buttressed by their determination, their gritty endurance, and in moments of self doubt, by their droll, dry wit so often kindly meant but equally, at times, a devastating weapon in the social armoury. They were the qualities of a spare countryside and they are binding on the soul.

WHERE the old croft stood by the narrow metalled ribbon that united the douce calm of Tarves with the venerable toon of Oldmeldrum it is a different dwelling that now claims the roadside, and maybe that is as it should be for the small croft 'shifts' – the small, patchwork fields – have long been subsumed into the acreage of the hilltop farmtoun that coveted them. The golden barley waves expansively in the vast single field they and the acres of adjoining crofts have become in a way it never did in my grandfather's time. The combine clanks efficiently round it in its season without that old fever of 'hairst' and without the tingle in the blood the old crofter men felt. Time and agri-chemicals and an abundance of subsidies have altered all that the old man held dear. I mind him well for I spent much of my childhood trailing at his heels, absorbing his wisdom and maybe just a little of his iron will. He was a man in the mould of his time; a dour man they say, and that even in the eyes of his children, who felt he had little time for them and that indeed may have been literally true, for he spent the week away at his mason's trade, returning to 'ca tae' the croft work in the last blink of daylight on Saturday afternoons. In his retirement and in the company of the grandbairn born in his house he was a different man, catching up perhaps with what had earlier been denied to him. He loved his 'bit grun', ill though it used him; it was like a hunger at the heart of him. In the winter evenings he read Pratt's Buchan as though it were a manual to some strange and distant land though he had worked and travelled every inch of it. It would have been strange indeed had his deep love of that countryside not communicated itself to the bairn.

It was a landscape of elemental values. I imbibed them, along with a love of its creatures, seated between him and my other retired grieve grandfather in the sheltering arbour the crofter man had made and set beside his bee hives to face the westering sun. Together they took stock of the countryside while I sat silent, listening to the slow interplay of their voices. Both were hard men who had handled squads of workers in their time but the years had mellowed them, making them no longer judgemental. Their 'news' would be punctuated by pondering silences, the scraping and filling of Stonehaven pipes, the tamping and igniting of Bogie Roll tobacco by fleering matches, the long pulls, the shaking of drottel. They looked out, the two of them, on a world they had helped to create. Sympathy – an ingrained understanding of all the hardships and injustices of the land – laced their talk as the last of the day's sun streaked the sky. From the arbour their gaze could sweep a wide panorama: figures in distant parks moved silently to some mysterious mantra of nature; closer, there might come the shout of some horseman as he 'lowsed' out of the plough for the day, the jingle of theats being unhooked from the swingle trees.

'Robbie's nae makin' muckle of the Little Mains.' In the pause their sorrow was palpable.

'No, he's nae that, puir chiel.'

'Puir grun, ye ken.'

'Coorse grun, richt enough.'

'He's weel ben at the bank, they say '

'Aye, likely so...He took her, they say, wi' little enyeuch siller.'

There was in that old farmtoun landscape a desire not to speak ill of those less fortunate; to find a loophole through which a reputation might slip without damage. In such conversations there lay a lesson for the listening bairn, as they rose, straightening work-worn joints, in the last of the light. 'Aye weel, we'll need tae see gin we're tae get some supper,' the crofter man would say, stepping stiffly towards the house, where the narrow stairs led up to wood lined garrets and the candle, guttering on its wall shelf whiles in the draughts if the night was stormy, illuminated your retirement under the warmth of thick Montgarrie blankets. Prayers were said, blessings earnestly sought, and the po used for the last time and pushed under the bed. On moonlight nights you could watch the lower clouds scudding across the skylight, or on a night of wind and wet watch the blattering raindrops runnel on the pane. It is landscape haunted still by the folk I once knew: the horsemen and bailies, orramen and maidservants of the old farmtouns with their infinite capacity for hard drudgery and, when it was needed, a deep compassion. It was a countryside that gave the 'daftie' a home and whiles managed to accord him a dignity that life had denied him. It was a land that comforted the widow and seldom spoke slightingly of the bastard bairn. Children came into it and were welcomed (the doctor fetched through the winter drifts by farm cart and willing teams of shovelling men); folk as suddenly left it for the infirmary by hasty ambulance down the rutted farm road, sometimes finally and forever, and more slowly, in the pneumatic ease of Montgomerie's motor hearse as their long day ended. Death was given its due regard in that far landscape for it lurked in every close: scarlet fever closed down the schoolroom, the diphtheria regularly awakened dread; strong men failed to rise from beds of pleurisy and pneumonia and tuberculosis hovered always in the shadows. As they passed from the only world they had known, those humble hard working folk, the countryside paid them its homage: awed bairns were summoned in from their play and the blinds were drawn. If some of them looked down they must have been surprised by the solemnity shown them by a society that seldom revered a man in his lifetime and if it did, in its broad humour, made damnably sure he never got too much above himself.

MAYBE I was fortunate in my cottared parents: my father was a sociable man who liked to play elaborate hoaxes on his fellow horsemen and my mother shared in the fun with a similar, impish, sense of mischief. Our cottar's house was endlessly full of folk. It was, after all, a sociable society that which barrowed turnips constantly through countless fattening byres and drew unending furrows in the fields. Often you could be hard pressed to get a seat in your own house. Our hearth, banked well up the chimney with peats and 'cinders' to spread a blanketing warmth round the kitchen, drew a motley crew.

Horsemen whose earlier fees to the same toun had cemented a friendship cycled over uninvited on their idle nights to 'hae a news an' see foo ye were', coming to the point of their errand if they had one hours later, baring their souls over trouble with their grieves, those masterful bossmen whose task it was to make thin ground bear riches, or some lass that had spurned their advances. But some came just for the fun of it, sure of a cup of cocoa and a butter biscuit before they took back to their cold chaumers. They were all of them characters, men with distinctive (and sometimes disgusting) traits that would have singled them out in any company. Lang Dod MacAllister had crossed my folk's cottared path on several occasions. A tall, lugubrious man with enormous feet and gangly legs that took up most of the hearth rug, which he monopolised without embarrassment, he had ears to match and a slack mouth that seemed forever flecked with spittle and on the edge of uttering an obscenity. Lang Dod was, as they said in the old speak, 'a hallyrakit breet'; his laugh too was like the rest of him and was almost in itself an offence. His heart was good, my mother swore, and maybe it was, but as for the rest of him, you would have said he had gotten the spare bits that nobody else wanted.

At one time the local bobby, too, was a regular visitor, coming in late from the night with a bottle or two of stout. A one time horseman (though I never heard it for sure), he sat well into the small hours and long after I had been ordered through to my bed in the ben-end. I would lie striving to keep awake, listening to the buzz of conversation and the occasional wild shriek of laughter, speculating on whether we were under suspicion or whether the man sprawled unbuttoned and claiming my father's chair by the hearth should have been out in the mirk fingering the collars of Haddo's poachers. Maybe indeed that's where he went when the door sneck finally fell behind him.

Whiles, now and then, some halflin loon once befriended and now shaved as we had never seen him before, would bring some shy kitchen 'deemie', his solemnly intended, for our inspection, ready at last to make permanent a relationship that would give him a cottar house of his own and after the appalling squalor of bothy life his own bed and board. As the evening wore on and my mother masked some tea and set out buttered, fresh-baked bannocks and some slices of seedcake the talk might take a turn to hilarity and the other benefits he might enjoy would be slyly alluded to, bringing a blush to the face of the bride. The speak, though risqué, was never coarse; foul mouthed obscenity would not have been tolerated, my mother would have seen to that.

At some time in his past bothy days my father – himself a dapper man – had acquired a set of hand clippers and with them a more than passable skill in the use of them. This too brought folk to our door; acquaintances rather than close friends driven by need; they stepped in with their bonnets in their hands to be seated and shorn in the circle of the hearth. The 'news' on such occasions was serious and polite, sometimes unbearably sad as a man, head bowed under the clipper, explained. 'My mother's funeral the morn, ' he would say and for a moment the kitchen quiet would be broken only by the snip snip of the scissors. But there were happier times: horsemen and bailies came from far farmtouns to be trimmed up for weddings (sometimes their own, glancing anxiously up every time the door opened, in dread that they had been followed by bothy colleagues intent on a feet-washing) and for christenings (in that old countryside the one followed quickly on the other), unexpected callers the cottar child could well endure for while it would have been unthinkable to offer the barber a fee it would have been unseemly to leave without pressing a sixpence into the bairn's palm. My father, I suspect, got his payment on Saturday nights, in the village inn.

BUT my parents' cottar life had its tensions. As the Term Days, Whitsunday and Michaelmas, drew near there was anxiety even for the cottar's bairn: would it be a new school soon and strange playmates, or the same school and the same pals joined down some other farm road? In the Depression Thirties farmers were cutting wages with every feeing fair, playing and maybe profiting as employers always do on the labourer's fears. There were plenty of folk in that now distant countryside for whom 'wark' was their only salvation for the cottar's life was one lived close to the bone, and well the farmers knew it. Some themselves were closely 'grippit' by the same hard times. As the Term Day drew ever nearer the concern mounted; daily without fail as he came in to his 'denner' my mother would ask my horseman father whether the farmtoun grieve had 'said onything'. These were fraught days and their inhumanity has been set down elsewhere. The farm servant's pride forbade that he should go cap in hand to ask about his future and finally as May or November approached it could become cruelly clear to a horseman or bailie that he 'wasnae bein' socht' and would soon be on his way down the farm road.

Usually, and belatedly, with little time to spare, my father would step in through the door for his noon meal and somewhere between the broth and breid and the rice pudding let fall casually (for that was his way) that he had been 'speired tae bide'. 'An' what said ye, man?' my mother would ask, her voice scarcely hiding her relief. 'Oh, I said tae him, "Fairly, I'll consider it, like, and mebbe there'll be a pound or twa mair in the year".' In truth, and both of them knew it, the room for manoeuvre was nil. The labourer was at the mercy of the master and, as with much else in my northern childhood, those days have remained with me and have moulded my political thinking for all of my life.

ON THOSE Term Days when we weren't 'flitting' that is, on the road with all our worldly belongings piled high on two carts and between one toun and the next it was my father's notion usually that he would spend his one day holiday by 'takin' a turn intae the toon'. Sometimes he would take me with him: we waited, chilled at the farm road end, by some sheltering hedge for the once a day bus to appear, taking a precautionary pee as it hove over the horizon. When it came it was already crowded and probably highly unsafe; there was no question of how many were allowed standing but of whose lap were you sitting on. The degree of intimacy that day didn't bear thinking about.

We decanted in Dee Street, the bus springs audibly sighing as the wheel arches eased up off the tyres, into a melee of country folk who, now that they were there, seemed to have nowhere to go. They were strangers in the city, suddenly out of their element, a lost look on their faces as they milled round the bus stance, unwilling to leave it and seizing the most tenuous acquaintance as an excuse for staying with other folk of their kind. With brittle laughter they at last ventured off reluctantly over the causey stones for the boulevard grandeur of Union Street.

Many would wander aimless through the throngs, ending their day disastrously in the bars of the Gallowgate and being sick on the bus home; others had ritual once a year ports of call: Raggie Morrison's and Isaac Benzie's and maybe the Fifty Shilling Tailor's near the Queen (if your Sabbath suit had seen better times) or maybe Esslemont and Mac's (if you were a lass with pretensions).

My father's itinerary could be more eclectic, depending on the weather, but (in my company) would always include the wonder of Woolies (its toys, ranked in serried rows, sumptuous and unattainable) followed by a wander in the New Market, 'a dander roon,' he would say, 'afore oor mince and tatties' in which my eager appetite was invariably badly blunted by the odour of blood and sawdust, the clash of meat cleavers and the sides of raw beef dangling from meat hooks. Sausages were strung like bunting above those counters of such bloody butchery and shivering mounds of brawn sat ponderous as Buddhas on white assiettes. There was something unsavoury about the New Market's first floor, as there was about its gallery, where young quines with black ringled een lounging in the doorways would look meaningfully at my father and some tink like jad, at the last, might accost him with: 'Three for yer Saiturday nicht, dearie?' 'Na, lassie, na faith ye. Thank ye,' he would say with his broad humoured grin; long it would be before I kenned what it was that was being offered him.

THEN it would be time for Torry. My father had a coven of aunts in Torry, country lasses who for good or ill had fallen for the charms of town men or the splendid availability of so many picture houses. All of them lived in a constant state of acrimony in the same tenement, Bell and Mary and the termagant Meg. They vied boisterously among themselves as to who would give us tea. Meg would brook no argument but that the honour was hers as the senior sister, which never surprised me for Meg was a substantial figure and ruled like a despot. Secretly though I would be delighted; from her top floor window I would be able to watch the trawlers with their gull shitten sides slide home through the sanctuary of Girdleness. Auntie Meg, I suspect, may have had some connection with the fish market. She laid a fine table for high tea, but invariably it featured yellow haddie so full of bones that they tested all my father's skill and defeated me completely. 'He's nae muckle of a feeder, is he?' Meg would say, watching my feeble performance and unable to curb her customary forthrightness. My father would give me discreet nods of encouragement but eventually end up lying bravely. 'He's nae muckle o' a loonie for fish, ye ken.' 'Ah weel,' Meg would say bleakly, her stare plainly indicting me for the insult to her fish, 'he'll likely nae hae room for ony of the fancies then!' Thus was the naked steel of the rapier thrust triumphantly between the ribs.

In the tall gaunt tenement Auntie Meg's household shared the indoor lavvy with six other families. It's flushing pan was then quite beyond the experience of the cottar's bairn, who grew up with the po or at best the pail below the board in some draughty outhouse, the latter only for serious business; under dry conditions the manly thing when in the grip of nature was to head out for the back and the nearby wood or (were it in reasonable proximity) to the stackyard. Truly, for the farmtoun bairn the flush toilet was a revelation and on my first such visit when I was barely started school and still having trouble with the spaver buttons of my best breeks Cousin Lily was deputed to accompany me down the dark terror of the stairs to the closet. There, unabashed and with a conspiratorial giggle, Cousin Lily deftly undid me and pointed me, so to speak, in the right direction while nestling my head against the yielding softness of her thighs, warm through the stuff of her flapper frock. I cannot say what experience Cousin Lily had had of such occasions but for the cottar's bairn it was a first encounter of such intimacy, only dimly understood.

On later visits I managed the lavvy on my own but for years after, whenever Auntie Meg and her brood visited for Sunday tea, Lily and I would exchange warm glances; we understood each other. Lily, I have to say, was careless with her frock, twining and twisting her legs in the chair to expose apricot underwear and once, to my blushes, a fair portion of hosed and gartered thigh. As we waved them off home and came in from the step my mother would say tartly: 'Lily's fast. She's afa in need o' a man.' My father would nod reluctant agreement but nothing more would be said and I was never told why.

ONCE a year we had another outing, a splendid jaunt in style to which we were certainly not accustomed. Unfailingly and with regularity and on a Sunday that fell between the haytime and the onslaught of harvest my crofting grandfather booked a hired car for the annual odyssey upcountry to my grandmother's folk in Montgarrie. It was I think his special treat to my grandmother, but given the expense it would have been a pity not to fill the car. Letters of confirmatory intent ('gin we a' be spared') would be sent out weeks beforehand and in time brought letters of reply suggesting at least that our visit was to be expected. The car would be ordered, and with it the driver, and doubtless some bargain struck between him and the crofter man (out of everyone's hearing and not disclosed to us), the account to be rendered and settled some time around Martinmas. Never did sahib set out more eagerly for Srinagar. For the cottar's bairn it was a day of high excitement such as might require a stop, mid route, at some convenient roadside wood, for he seldom rode in a car never mind the luxury of such a luxurious saloon. Johnnie's car was indeed a fine limousine, quite the best for miles around not excluding the few rich farmers' equipages and went to all the good funerals. Seated in its grandeur we thought few our equal that day but, mindful of the morrow, were careful to give a wave in passing to such acquaintances as we met on the road. A nod of recognition sufficed for folk we might otherwise have wrung by the hand.

The vehicle was so grossly overloaded that I marvel now that it did not overheat or strip a crown and pinion; bodies squeezed five on to a seat meant for three and every lap carried an additional burden, one of them the bairn. There would have been high hilarity at the back had we not, the most of us, been a bit overawed by the occasion. My grandfather, in his best and only tweed suit, sat in the front as was his right, eyes apprehensively on the road and exchanging pleasantries with the driver but in truth a bit grim faced and obviously anxious for like the bairn he was rarely in a car, his velocity along the turnpike being limited to what could be induced from the pedals of his bicycle. All the same, it was a fine day... a day of upcountry 'news' and good humour with maybe a pot-roast for lunch and a few fancies for tea and by the time it came the hour to leave, Johnnie, who sat always on a hard chair in the corner, no doubt conscious of the fact that he was not of the family circle, had become like a member of it.

Quietly on the return run through the summer night there would percolate the moments of thoughtful reflection ('Nellie's frailer nor she was'/'Margit's loon is a bonnie laddie, like his father wid ye say?') but eventually these too would trail into a silence as cushioned rubber smoothed the homeward miles and the only debate was 'will we need lichts?'. Johnnie, again now the professional chauffeur, would set us down by the croft's door, politely refusing yet another cup of tea (and no doubt exhausted by a family that strove and bickered and laughed and talked so ferociously through each other) and headed for home. For once there would be unanimity that it had been 'a richt fine day'. The bairn, tired though he was, could hardly wait to get to school the next day to tell his friends...

A CROFT they say was never a viable agricultural unit; what it was, was a home, a hub for the family, and certainly my grandfather's holding like our cottar's house was a great gathering point. Folk converged from all directions, sometimes not waiting for an invitation but appearing suddenly on the flimsiest pretext. There could be three sittings at my grandmother's Sabbath lunch table, stretching late into the afternoon and to the chagrin, I can tell you, of those who were there by filial right, for her excellent pot roast would be strained to go round. My grandfather, presiding with some dignity at the head of his board, would have to carve thinly and the first course broth would have to be surreptitiously watered, yielding fewer carrots than were enough to go round. With his guests in the circumstances as well fed as possible there would be semolina to follow the old crofter man would lead the male contingent out into his small cornyard (on fine days) or (in winter) into the shelter of the byre, where he housed always one milk cow and a couple of fattening stirks. Pipes would be lit, undue flatulence relieved and opinions frankly aired. It was my grandfather's way, folk said, to ask everybody's advice and then damn well please himself.

Perched on the milk stool taken down from its peg on the wall, the cottar bairn made his first tentative acquaintance with the company of men and acquired a working knowledge of some words he would not hear in the house; he would watch the poor stots having their sides prodded and their haunches slapped as assessment was made of their condition. 'They'll put on a bit o' beef, Wullie, fin ye get them oot tae the girss.' The crofter would nod sagely. 'Haud the neeps at them, man,' would be the advice of another. Wullie would nod again, just as sagely. Somebody would hold his Sabbath jacket while he ran besom along the greep to swill the morning's sharn through the byre's wall chute into the adjoining midden.

In truth, for a crofter family, our social circle was wide, from immediate relatives to those of the most tenuous acquaintance. To my grandfather's holding, all summer long, came all manner of folk from all over the globe: from distant corners of Africa that have changed their names a dozen times in my lifetime even from Australia and the snowy wastes of Winnipeg. I had 'uncles' everywhere trying to make an honest living or reform the world; some took their entrepreneurial skill, some took the Word. Willie Park's superior store in Calgary sent its yearly calendar of a red faced outdoor man pulling a bucking salmon from some torrent in the dominion on bending rod and taut line, with his emporium's motto proudly emblazoned on it: 'Hooked on a fair deal'. The lad from Portlethen had learned a thing or two on his way across the great wheat plains.

Sons and daughters of surrounding crofts and farmtouns, known since they had first trailed reluctantly past on their way to school, would be invited for their supper and to take a dram with the crofter man, who kept a bottle always handy but was, said his sons in law, sometimes loth to broach it. They were all of them entertaining folk for the bairn allowed to sit on the 'clickit' rug at their feet before the blaze of the parlour fire. Their 'news' continued late, till my grandfather convoyed them into the night and some distance on their way, as though unwilling to let them go. (It was the custom of the old crofter's house that all guests had to be 'convoyed' – accompanied – for the first half mile or so home as part of their leave-taking; anything less and you would have known that your visit had been less than welcome.) The talk that night would be magical, for the bairn a breath of beckoning other worlds. Some of the croft guests were indeed missionaries in the Dark Continent, taking our homely gospel to the heathen hordes who were, by all accounts, more amenable and less in need of it than some of the farmtouns' horsemen. They were dedicated folk who would return home in time, some of them with nervous breakdowns, their Aberdeenshire grit temporarily eroded by the enormity (and maybe the thanklessness) of their task.

There was a time in my childhood – or so it seemed – when the farm-toun lads, tired of their unremitting round of toil, were all 'lifting their kists' from their cheerless chaumers to escape their charted fates in the ranks of the Metropolitan police force. A fine body of men it must have been then, with so many 'stoot chiels' in it. Most took to the life like ducks to the farm dam, their slow voices adding a dour and ponderous authority to the uniform and doubtless causing alarm and despondency in the breast of any Cockney ne'er-do-well who suddenly felt the grip of their ploughman's hands on their collar and perhaps a flutter of real apprehension as he was advised: 'Come ye awa' noo wi' me, mannie, doon tae the clink.' After the ploiter of work in the winter fields the job must have seemed like a holiday to them: they waxed fat and prosperous, found their strangely incorruptible characters worthy of quick promotion and bought houses in the capital's green suburbs and sent their daughters to university. Lasses of the farmtouns, fearing a life of like servitude or maybe a future as crofters' wives, took their bonnie looks and down-to-earth natures into the wider service of medicine and in time, too, found their way to the capital's great citadels for the sick, catching a surgeon instead.

Few, though, forgot who they were, the roots that nourished them: they came home for the hairst and the haytime to help out with the work, able still to bind and stook and fork to the cart with the same adroitness with which they could now bandage a wound for these were the inborn skills of a northern childhood and never left them. They would come to afternoon tea in our cottar house those friends of my mother's childhood to sip daintily from our Sunday china and talk with a reckless amusement of their life 'in theatre' and all the ills and ailments that folk were heir to, the male genitalia as familiar to them now as a farm graip. They wore flapper frocks and silk hose and high heels and for the cottar bairn clutched fondly to their cleavages the smell of them was a drug on the senses.

Whiles they came home, these quines with their daily acquaintance with all male appendages, demure as brides with their finally-intendeds – men from another planet ill at ease in that bare and wind-scoured countryside and with folk who took the size of a man in an instant. They struggled bravely, all the same, those young and dapper lads with jammy bannocks and unswallowable seedcake and heroically drank my grandmother's strong tea; mostly they had to have the conversation translated to them but they were 'fine enough chiels' my grandfather would say, for all that, when he had bidden them 'Guidnicht'.

Letters would come for my mother from time to time; what they said, like the topics of the afternoon tea talk, was a mystery never explained to me. Some, I suspect now, were the sad chronicles of blighted love affairs ('He's marriet,' my mother might say, tersely and obliquely to my father as we sat at the supper table). But married, they would fail in time to return for the harvests of the year, vanishing forever into the bridge circuits of Surbiton or Esher.

In such social rituals the cottar's bairn absorbed many things – the things that would stay with him and leaven his life, not least the unpredictability of existence, the value of acquaintance, the worth of genuine, warm friendship as well as its fragility maybe most of all, a loyalty to his kind. Somewhere among those kenspeckle folk he learned the gift of easy laughter as well as the sorrow of its transience. Above all, I believe, he absorbed from those people of the old crofts and farmtouns the marvellous nature of life itself and the need to respond to it. And yet another precious thing he learned and learned quickly whether in the village school playground or playing among the ricks of the twilight cornyard was how to rub along with the rest of the world and, in particular, some of the old cottar's skill in bargaining from a position of disadvantage without himself acknowledging it.

WE WERE kirk going folk; God was not mocked in that old landscape nor was His name taken vainly. Strong men went out of their way to ameliorate their expressions of irritation or surprise with a modulated 'Dyod' rather than offend. (It was Dyod this and Dyod that, and even now, in an increasingly hedonistic world where the Church trims frantically at its sails to meet the needs of a vacuous society, I am unhappy if I find myself transgressing.) The Lord was all powerful, the keeper of our lives and I have never forgotten it. The links are enduring. If I am now seldom in a church – inexplicably one loses the habit while being conscious of the loss – be it kirk or chapel I never enter without being aware of the odour of sanctity that resides there as it did in the plain little country kirk our family attended.

The Sabbath morning, like the Term Days, saw the roads lively with folk, clutching Bible and gloves, lengthening their step anxiously at the first toll of the kirk bell. We were like the Jews, we walked, as did many other families, meeting at my grandfather's croft before setting out *en famille*. On a fine Sabbath morning the old man would be in fine humour as he stepped through his beloved countryside taking stock of beast and crop. Plants of the road verge would be identified for the bairn, who pulled the flowers off them and brought them for his closer study; trees were named for his benefit, 'yowies' (fir cones) gathered and stuffed into his jersey pockets. Nature, after that, would never be a stranger to him. On such days ('A fine hairst day,' the men would say stoically one to the other, not daring then to make it so), if we had made good speed, there would be time to linger in the warm sun amid the gravestones. There in the kirkyard was identity more firmly imprinted; the Mafia itself could not have more strongly instilled the sense of family.

'Yer great grandfather,' the bairn would be told, pausing before some dark, lichened stone that recorded no more than a name and the sum of his days, for our family was sparing of public ostentation. Unseemly it would have seemed to us to leave lamenting messages for posterity; I cannot tell you now whether anyone loved him or if he came there unmourned.

'He wis gey fond o' the bottle,' my grandmother might confide quietly, for he wasn't *her* father. Pause might be made before a stone but newly erected, the name read, pronounced solemnly off the lips, and a moment of silence observed before the crofter man spoke.

'Yon would be a Lorimer of Peathill, surely?'

'Na, Man.' My grandmother would be emphatic. 'I would nae think so… Peathill nivver had nae sons o' that name that ivver I heard o'.'

'Is that so, noo, Umman.' For so, in such primal terms, he always addressed her.

'Nivver that ivver I heard tell o', Man,' she would say. Their lives had a Biblical simplicity. The crofter man, filling his pipe for a pre-sermon draw, would look bleakly round God's acre, slowly filling with all the folk he had known, before retorting with ill grace: 'Weel, weel, Umman. Gin that be the case I kenna whar he's a Lorimer fae.' And so our small party, bathed in gentle and unexpected sunlight, moved on, circumnavigating the sacred ground, each with the expectation that one day they too would come to lie there.

So the cottar's bairn learned that sadness of death that was in life: under the stones lay an army of folk that were kin to him, whose name he might carry, whose dour and awkward blood ran in his veins – those who had been poor in spirit, spinsters harshly used, ploughmen who had turned long and endless furrows and never been champions; folk from both sides of the blanket who had been neither worse nor better than they'd had to be, finally at peace, their sins forgiven though not forgotten.

My grandfather's rented pew was up the steep stone side-stair, in the kirk loft. Seated on its bare board we looked down aslant on the pulpit and on the minister's thinning pow – and were badly discomfited when he suddenly glowered round on us, indicting us of some unstated sin. Below us too was the choir stall and the generous shadowed cleavage of its star, Miss Wilson, who sang proud as a linnet and come Monday would be winsomely back behind the baker's counter to sell you 'a pennyworth of brokens'. Through the loft's oriel windows darted beams of the mellow sunlight in which the moths danced iridescent; beyond them the Sabbath quiet of the land lay unbroken but for the call of a bird or the distant bark of a dog. Into that holy and healing silence there came too from time to time the faint reeshle of the bag of pandrops that came quietly out of the old man's pocket and made its surreptitious passage along the pew – to be returned as discreetly. The crofter man, I believe, was inclined to fall asleep during the sermon for his religion, like that of so many of the men of that northern land, was the 'grun' and his sweeties were a ploy to keep him awake.

All the same, the Sabbath was holy and we kept it. However hard the itch to 'hairst', however deep the need, the parks that day were still and empty of folk. There were men of the crofts and farmtouns who that day would not put a brush to their byre greeps; their beasts got fed and milked and were given leave to lie in their own mess till Monday. The Sunday broth would simmer through Saturday (and need only warming up) and the 'tatties' sat peeled on the bink, ready for salting and boiling when we came in from the kirk. That day the bairn put away childish things: his catapult, his pluffer and his Meccano set.

THE Thirties cottar's bairn was born into a different wor
ent landscape, a country society more integrated thar
again. I early imbibed its sounds and smells as well as its
ents' cottar house in the toun they fee'd home to after I was
the middle of the 'closs', the farm yard; I lay in my pram at its door
ing the dust of the harvest sheaves as they came home to the cornyard
and on the heels of that the fine pungent odour of the dung as it was carted out from the midden in the autumn. The kye coming in for the afternoon milking (my mother once told me) would pause on their leisurely way to look in on me before passing on, no doubt excreting liberally. I was the last of my family to be born into that life and I remember it and its folk with affection. There is a nostalgia still for its ordered structure, for its close ties and not least for its sounds: the jingle of traces in the November dusk as the toun's horsemen came home from the plough; the *clank* of the binders in the golden glow of a harvest day; for the *scrunch* of the iron runged carts as they swayed and lurched home on the rutted farm road with their turnip loads; the *brumm brumm* of the barn mill as the water went on for the weekly 'thrash'. They return on some stray and wandering wind of the mind, where they have long been harboured, those things that gave my young life significance and have now been embellished by the years.

I have watched from the sidelines the disappearance of that world before the unrelenting march of mechanised farming, which would transform the countryside and in doing so destroy everything the old countrymen held dear; shattering the flow of the seasons and the patterns of the year that gave a meaning to *their* lives. Those old patterns of the land – the grid of hay coles and stooks that stood to the sun, the cluster of ricks in the cornyard – were linked inextricably with the subliminal lessons of my young life (as they were with every other cottar bairn's) for they placed man reassuringly in the landscape: he fitted with nature, coercing and cajoling her like a wooer. Now that unfolding panorama has been swept away. Machines would allow man to impose his will in a way undreamed of. But at a cost: he would slowly and forever distance himself from the soil, from the thing that sustained him, seeking a facile fulfilment in an increasingly industrial (and now technological) milieu that would offer him only the heady materialism of its spoils. I cannot think man has profited by the deal. In his future age he would become as ard-edged as the tools he honed in his Midlands factory.

Only those born in the bosom of the land would truly know the deprivation, adapting as best we could, ceaselessly forced to shift our horizons to meet the brittle future. There is something depressingly desolate about today's countryside devoid of the harvesters', hoers' and tattie gatherers' voices; about the lonely parks – that loneliness only emphasised by the staccato crackle of the diesel's exhaust. They have kicked away the scaffolding on which so many once built their lives.

IT IS the heritage of the Thirties bairn that he was born to straddle two cultures, the old and the new. His was the last generation to know the ballad as well as the plough. The horse would fade as the land's icon, usurped by the iron monsters made in Minneapolis and Detroit, and with it the society that surrounded it. It was not, perhaps, a polite society; how could it be with so much deprivation and exploitation? We see the scars that life inflicted in the solemn sepia'd faces that stare back at us from the prints the camera has preserved from that time: it is the look of the peasant everywhere – as much Calabrian or Sicilian – that stares back at us, raw and naked to the world, for it was not their way to dissemble as the calculating and knowing dissemble. Dressed in their cords and heavy kerseys, they face the lens without flinching and I am moved by their stoicism.

Such then were the images, the memories, the emotional burdens the cottar's bairn took with him into his future years. There was loss as well as gain. In his heart he would carry the old speak of his northern landscape but find its cherished richness denied to him, impoverishing him in a society where the *lingua franca* of his Aberdeenshire childhood must at best be transmuted into no more than a regional burr, at worse buried forever in his subconscious. His native Doric would not take him farther than Montrose. He must needs discard the rich pearls that fell so easily from his grandparents' lips and re-equip himself with the peely-wally baubles of a southern tongue. Yet there was one positive benefit for the cottar's bairn in the language of his old countryside: it qualified hope and expectancy with a hesitancy born of long disillusionment that made disappointment all the more bearable and triumph sweetly unalloyed.

Mindful of that, the Thirties child went forth aware of life's uncertainties. If it fettered him, it also gave him a healthy doubt about yielding too easily to euphoria. He became a man loth to count chickens.

And the Thirties bairn was heir to yet another inheritance, not to be discounted, one that soldered him to the past and the country he came from; he was the late legatee of that great body of song, the bothy ballads, the raucous minstrelsy of those single horsemen's barracks where the hardship was such that its inmates fled for the comfort of army life. He would be the last of his kind to hear those songs sung in the context of the society that begat them to the ill buttoned notes of a wheezy melodeon and the scraich of a wild fiddle, rather than in their cultural revival on a National Trust open afternoon. Their repertoire of work and wooing are enshrined in the heart. I have hummed the dirding tune of the 'Barnyards' (my father's favourite as he plotted some mischief) or 'Drumdelgie' in the middle of a London traffic snarl and felt sane again.

Like their photographs, the ballads tell us much about the folk who sang them. Today we seek the voice of their retreating landscape and pen portraits of its sinewy, argumentative folk in the works of William Alexander, where Johnny Gibb is an archetypal figure; in the prose of such writers as David Toulmin, recounting at first hand the old close relationship with the land; or in the deeply informed poetry of Flora Garry or John C. Milne whose work perpetuates the rich seam of language as well as that northern psyche that springs from the very earth itself. For the exile they are the sources in which he periodically touches base. Does anyone else, I wonder, take down Murray from the shelf on a grey suburban Sunday and savour that great ode to northern childhood, 'It Wasna His Wyte', recited it so many school concerts? Or slipping from some London tavern to hail a taxi while the hour is still discreet, relish momentarily in the mind the humour of his home going elder in 'A Cheery Guid Nicht':

> Rowe garvits weel roon, an' your bonnets rug doon,
> Syne set the door wide to the wa',
> An' the gig that's in front is the safest to mount,
> Gin the dram gars you trow there is twa.

In 'The Hint of Hairst' he longs for home, as must every exile. In 'Jeemes' he faces the reality of death in that elemental landscape – as a necessary part of life, giving the act a quiet, unfussy piety, a spare and moving dignity that was ever part of that countryside. Death lacked all ostentation and was the better for it; heads that bowed as bonnets were doffed, as they took a man out for his last journey past the parks he had tended, said more unsaid than the elaborate rituals of other creeds and races. That too was something the cottar's bairn intuitively realised, watching discreetly from the corner of the byre or the barn gable. Murray parades for our later time so many of the country's characters: the miller, the packman, the precentor, tink and grave-digger. Few poets people the land so well.

Yet if that old landscape has an emblem figure it is surely that of the horseman, a man immersed sometimes in his own secret culture. His endless solitary furrow, drawn through the dreich end days of October and November on the stubble – he would move with the New Year on to the ley ground, its 'furs' gleaming richly dark as they fell from the mouldboard – is a metaphor for life itself. The horse plough was heavy with symbolism and another Aberdeenshire exile, arguably more famous than Murray, the Auchterless crofter's boy Lewis Grassic Gibbon, was not unaware of it. His finest homage to the land whose rhythms he would so successfully subsume into his art – his 'land out there, under the sleet, churned and pelted there in the dark' – is his confession: 'I like to remember I am of peasant rearing and peasant stock.' He added: 'Good manners prevail on me not to insist on the fact overmuch.' But who among us has not in a svelte and sophisticated age felt a need at times for the heartsome smell of dung? As he did.

●

SO THE Aberdeenshire bairn imbibed the precepts of life, and a set of values so inbred in him that he could never forget them. He would take them with him into the groves of learning, medicine, the church, policing, engineering and a whole raft of other professions and to lands all over the globe – strangely sure of himself, an irritating trait for those who might associate with him.

I have worked in a world where egos were regularly – even as a matter of policy – demolished overnight; where those with fragile identities could be heartlessly and humiliatingly destroyed. I have been thankful for that resilience bred in the bone, my inheritance from those folk who drove the Clydesdale pairs and mucked the byres and tended the little crofts that once clothed every northern hillside. I have emerged drained after a day of recycling the world's gloom into the lilac dusk of Fleet Street as the first editions began to roll and heard in my mind the restorative dird and thump of the bothy ballads; the cultivated veneer slips and the loon is hame. Those songs and the memories associated with them have lifted the heart on the short walk through the evening streets to Smithfield's car park, where the refrigerated meat lorries are already gathered, waiting for the market to open its gates to the night, the names emblazoned on their sides evoking a familiar countryside: Fraserburgh, Mintlaw, Inverurie, Tarves. Their drivers, relaxed, are trading the gossip of the day round one particular cab. Passing the burr of their voices – and catching their glances askant at the city suedes, the briefcase and business suit – I have been tempted to speir heartily: 'Aye, aye. An' foo are ye?'

I have not done so. But I have been deeply aware that even there on the rimed and treacherous cobbles of London's great market the bairn from that distant childhood is strangely linked with home. Today it is the refrigerated vans that converge there, but once, more romantically if less hygienically, it was the mecca of the old droving men. Beasts bought once at the great fair of Aikey Brae would wade Tangland Ford to join the big droves south to be sold at Norfolk's equally famous St Faith's for fattening for the capital's tables, and to come later, skittering through the night streets, into that great arena beside St Bartholomew's old kirk and venerable hospital. The old drove road they had taken ran past on the ridge behind the croft where I was born. On such nights, amid such scenes, the cottar's bairn has known who he was and never been in doubt of it. He has been acutely conscious of the resonances of that northern landscape and the roots that nourished him. Like Gibbon, he has felt a fierce pride to be of its sturdy peasant stock; unlike him, I fear, he may sometimes have been unforgivably ill-mannered about it.

TAE TRY AN' MAK SMA' SHAVES, O' FIT MAY BE THE TRUTH O'T[1]

Iain F W K Davidson

My recollections of childhood seem frequently to be set against a background of light. For most of my primary school years we lived at 178 Skene Street West, opposite the façade of the Grammar School, my visual image of which – from the top (second) floor – is of an imposing silver-grey, turreted and battlemented pile, clear in a cool light or sparkling in sunshine. A small effort alters the image to one of a duller grey, even sullen building, seen through rain, but an effort is required; what spontaneously occurs is a scene that is full of light. It is not the light that I later came to know and appreciate in Sicily, or Greece, warm and welcoming. Rather it is a light that has no hint of drama in it, no invitation to enter and bathe in it; it is a light of statement, even under-statement, and diffused. I had never realised that my memories of early childhood were so strongly imbued with light until I began writing this piece. Doubtless it has something to do with my spending my most exciting times outdoors, playing on the pavements and in the gardens and alleys around Skene Street West and in the school playground. It also, I think, has to do with the sense I had then, and now recall, of the endlessness of play, of utter absorption in matters of the moment. Whatever we were given to do by our parents and elders was natural, simply there, unquestioned, whether welcomed or not – school, meals, listening to the radio, going to church; but the naturalness had no qualifications when we played, even those of time.

I don't see childhood as idyllic, in general or in my case, but I do remember a different experiential sense, a 'feel' to what I was doing, an all-or-nothing, naturally occurring, unselfconscious participation in life's events. This made for high enjoyment and eager anticipation of many

[1]Extract from 'Gi' me the een again', W Gordon Lawrence

things. Play was our natural state; other activities might intrude or be a nuisance or unpleasant, but these we rarely chose, and for the most part they were out of our control. The playground was well named at school. As I look at my primary school, then called Queen's Cross Primary School, now a small office building, I have one sense as I look at the playground and another as I look at the classroom windows. The playground was a release from the classroom, the classroom an intruder on our proper playground-located activity, which we created, enhanced or spoiled at will but which *we* understood and which came naturally to us. And, as by far most play took place outdoors, in daylight, my memories are commonly of light.

The L-shaped space that was the playground now seems impossibly confining. The boys and girls played separately or squabbled together; the girls skipped, bounced balls or huddled in groups, while the boys raced around or played football against a wall – it seems someone always had a worn tennis ball. I remember little of the detail, but rather the intensity, the noise, the urgency, created by rushing, shouting, pushing, and showing off to the girls. The adrenaline flowed, but so occasionally did blood. There was little fighting, but the playground's being of tarmac and too crowded for free movement inevitably led to collisions with children or walls, stumblings and trippings over. In more dramatic cases, there followed the ceremonial summoning of a teacher, first aid and sympathy, and the accolade of injury in the form of a bandage, Elastoplast, or visible bump on the forehead. With luck the raw wound became a scar, to be looked at or even touched with expressions of fascinated disgust, and eventually to be picked at, as an interest in itself or as competitor for attention with the teacher's words.

Outside the playground, I experienced school as a 'serious' place, a place where a kind of business was being conducted that had to be important (even though I did not understand it) because the adults involved went about it in a serious way. Fun in the classroom came not from participating in the curriculum or demonstrating the behaviour required of us but from our pursuing our own agenda, to talk, fidget, tease, in short to bring the playground into the classroom. In our small school, we had only four classrooms with two or three age-groups in each. I can remember only three of the teachers to a reasonable extent, and the commonalties among them more than their respective individualities. They must have been in their forties or fifties, born before or just after the century began, and would have undertaken teacher training during or in the aftermath of World War One. Mother McGrory, the Headmistress, was from the Central Belt, Miss MacKenzie and Miss Ferguson from the North East, but all had, I think, taught only Aberdeen Catholic children. In all the classes I remember chanting – tables, spelling, catechism answers, poetry – and the efforts to learn by heart the contents of the chants, and I remember English and arithmetic exercises, and pages of ticks and crosses against my efforts. Reading books were well worn and often shared; we read aloud round the class. As a good reader I was allowed to read books from the small library, many (most?) of them of the improving sort, and was encouraged to join the Public Library. Writing was primarily required for exercises, though 'compositions' on given topics became important as we climbed up through the classes. Free writing of this sort, such as it was, allowed me to dilate on aerial dogfights and heroic soldiers, but we did not write journals nor do group work for projects. We did learn to punctuate, to various degrees of success, and we parsed. We wrote with pens dipped in inkwells; we copied the copperplate script at the head of each page, and tried to avoid blots by learning to lick our nibs before their immersion in ink, and by using blotting paper.

Art was not taught by a specialist, nor was music; we sketched and shaded vases, and we sang songs by heart to a piano, having laboured for years to follow a pointer moving up and down, in increasingly unpredictable order, a chart with Doh at the top and bottom. Physical education consisted of occasional supervised games in the neighbouring Convent grounds, or exercises conducted in the playground and sometimes in the classroom. I recall no investigation or use of the trees next to the school, or observation of the birds whose song penetrated the windows and whose nests could be seen through them. Nor were there trips to the museum or art gallery, possible even in wartime. We did, however, once form one bloc of flag waving children on Great Western Road, watching the King and Queen drive swiftly along en route to Balmoral. Discipline involved a good deal of stern-faced rebuking and use of the belt, both often communicated to parents, who seemed to us to stand united in unfair alliance with our teachers, and at times extended the punishment at home. There was no question of talking back or resistance, beyond, 'It wasn't me, Miss/Mother', as that increased the fault and the penalty; obedience was all. Both boys and girls were belted, the boys more often, lengthily and vigorously, and punishment was often in front of the class.

My summary account of remembered aspects of primary school does not differ greatly from others that I have read or heard from contemporaries regarding their early school days, in Scotland, the rest of Britain and beyond. My sense now is of a group of people, teachers, who felt strongly the responsibility of providing children with a societally imposed, agreed on but little examined curriculum, but who were neither appropriately educated nor trained for the work of teaching. At the very end of the twentieth century it is difficult to grasp the flavour of early twentieth century assumptions and conditions of education within which my early teachers had been taught and then trained, and within which my early schooling took place. Our teachers had been trapped into a perspective that focused on products – ability to read, knowledge of number bonds, addition, subtraction, multiplication and division, ability to put words on paper legibly, good behaviour – that would stand their pupils in good stead in earning a living and being good citizens. They may well have considered as valuable notions such as individual development, encouragement of strengths, individual interests and creativity, exploration of the environment and of local history and projects, but not had the confidence nor opportunity to pursue their own thinking.

As we reached the upper end of primary school we noticed that younger children were inferior beings, to be patronised and allowed to seek our attention, especially when we attained the pinnacle of Primary VII. Examinations neared and occupied the teachers hugely. As Catholic children we had been introduced to episodes of high seriousness in our preparation for first Confession and Communion, and later Confirmation. But before early Primary VII tests had been in-house matters; orders of merit had been established, reinforced, sometimes amended, carelessness had been criticised and punished, and laziness as a term had been made familiar to us all. Within the group, however, friendships and animosities mattered much more than intellectual boundaries and limitations. Now another set of truths took hold of us. Whatever terms were used in regard to individual children, no child was now left in any doubt about whether he/she was a success or a failure. Being a success meant that you went to Robert Gordon's College or the Grammar School, if you were a boy, or just possibly the Central School, which had a small proportion of boys in a largely girls' school. To it occasionally went one of the Queen's Cross girls, but most went to the Convent, our big, awesome neighbour occupying the corner of Queen's Road and St Swithin Street.

Failure meant that you went to a junior secondary school, thence to join the world of work long before your 'successful' primary school friends had to leave school, festooned with examination certificates. We had all absorbed notions of success and failure, clever/not clever, good/bad at school work as we climbed the classes, but it was only in Primary VII that our assent became more real than notional as our destinations became clear. Those of us considered 'clever' – the word was used by our teachers in class – basked in the glory, vaguely aware of some sort of good fortune that had come to us and somewhat (though not excessively) sorry for those of our classmates not so categorised. We were unceasingly reminded that more was expected of us, that we really had no right to make errors or be careless. I took this mostly in my stride, apart from one aspect. On several occasions I was singled out in class by Mother McGrory when I had achieved a high score in sums or written a good composition or done some such thing; so too were others, and it was not difficult to understand and enjoy such praise. But in Primary VI and VII the word 'ambition' was used to explain my achieving high marks, though no one, to my recollection, ever clarified it. I realised that it conveyed a great deal to the headmistress and that being ambitious – more precisely, having ambition – gave one a powerful advantage in school work and examinations and in achieving senior secondary school. At no time, however, did I identify anything in myself that I could recognise as ambition. If it meant 'wanting to get on', and at school that phrase was frequently used, I found no strong, intrinsic desire to do so, though I did wish to please my parents and relations. I remained uneasy about the ascription and had to settle for some sense of being a fraud, or rather of having fraudulence thrust upon me.

The Order of the Sacred Heart, originating in France, had opened a primary school in 1896, not long after it had established its own convent and girls' secondary school, and the Headmistress was always a nun.

Queen's Cross Primary occupied a corner of the Order's property at the junction of St Swithin Street and Queen's Road Lane; it was separated from the Convent's open play space in the 1940s by a thicket of trees, through which we could at times hear the girls at play. Across this open space we traipsed for Mass and air-raid drills, or the actuality of an air-raid, to enter what seemed cavernous halls, gloomy for blackout precautions and lack of windows. I can conjure up the visual image of a crowded long, low and dimly lit room, containing our whole school, perhaps sixty to eighty children, all trying to breathe through our gas masks, and finding it just possible but an effort. The rubbery smell was oppressive, reminding many of us of the school dentist's, but we found compensation in the gas mask's capacity to alter our voices to funny/scary ones similar to those we heard on Saturday mornings at the Mickey Mouse Club at the Odeon on Justice Mill Lane. The occasional glimpse of a gas-masked teacher was something to be cherished, perhaps because she looked awkward or ridiculous. The prime delight, however, was the ability of the gas mask to produce a farting sound, usually by sublime accident, but for a few pupils – inevitably boys – through the discovery of the right combination of breathing, placing of the rubber on the cheeks and chin, and persistence. And one could always claim lack of intention because of the awkwardness of the apparatus.

Mass in the Convent chapel was always, I think, shared with the Convent girls and staff, and had to do with Holy Days of Obligation, feast days of the Church when Mass was obligatory. My guess is that the whole school was taken to Mass to ensure that no pupil from a less than attentive family actually missed Mass, then considered a mortal sin, with the attendant and implacable penalties of fall from grace. It is difficult to convey now, (from the distance of over fifty years and a life-view that no longer includes a religious belief), the global sense of certainty, comfort, disaster or fear that many of us then experienced. We did not share this with adults. My mother's piety did not, I think, allow for any doubt: the Church was right at some level beyond question. I never heard her speak of her personal spiritual life, but my sense is that she put doubts and confusions and difficulties in understanding down to her own inadequacy and the human foibles of others, to be resolved only within God's master plan. That plan would – could – be known only after death. Our teachers' religious beliefs would have been of the same sort, I am sure, for I encountered this sort of thinking well into my adult life in fellow-Catholics and recognised both what it offered and what it denied to believers.

What our teachers personally thought was not shared with us, by and large, but their presentation of religious truth was constant, through religious instruction and observance in school. We learned by rote the answers to questions in the Catechism – Who made you? God made me. Why did God make you? To know Him, to love Him, to serve Him in this world, and to be happy with Him in the next. I'm not sure if I have remembered the words exactly, but I am struck by my reserving happiness for the next world and by the one-way effort implied in relating to God in this world, for these reflect very well the notion of God that permeated my childhood and of the sort of life that He expected us to lead. The Catechism was a conceptually sophisticated and dense document, encapsulating a rich belief system in relatively few words; it used a question and answer format familiar to schoolchildren. Unfortunately the concepts were beyond children's understanding. What did stick in my mind was communicated through the actions and reactions of our teachers and parents, and I didn't relate the world of behaviour to that of the Catechism because the latter was too abstract. Fifty years and more later, what I recall is a sense of there being a fixity to life, ways of being and behaving, thinking and feeling, a structuring, organising, directing, preventing principle in accordance with which I (and everyone else) should live. The rules to be followed, the areas and types of knowledge to be learned, the expectations to be met were seemingly crystal clear to adults, for they unambiguously let us know whether or not we were following the right paths.

The setting where I experienced the widest variety of religious behaviour was in church itself, specifically St. Mary's Cathedral in Huntly Street, our family's parish church, for two reasons. First, going to church, while a practice rooted in the inner family in which I lived my daily life and linked closely to the school life that I lived for over three-quarters of the year, nevertheless went far beyond the boundaries of both family and school. There I saw familiar people – relations, some neighbours, friends' parents, teachers – kneeling, standing, sitting, praying out loud, singing and processing, activities which I too carried out. I thus gained, through a sharing of special activities, a further sense of community with those I knew. Then, I gradually came to recognise many more people, as they appeared Sunday by Sunday, by their faces, their clothes ('Sunday best' is a term that I still associate with well-kept, familiar clothing), their walk (especially their footsteps), their mannerisms, their way of coughing and their unvarying place in church.

After Mass people gathered in chattering groups, under a haze of cigarette smoke, of family members, family friends and acquaintances. We children were ritually admired for growing so fast and asked how we were 'getting on' in school; the adults asked after absent men folk, commented on the weather and conversed, in every sense, above our heads. If my father were on leave he had much hand-shaking to do while my mother and we children stood proudly beside him in his uniform. But for us there were three years without a serving member of the family at home and the women of the family could only look on wistfully as other uniformed men stood with their families or, in strange uniforms, looked around at their foreign co-religionists whom they could barely understand, if at all.

The second, more particular, factor contributing to broadening my experience was that I became an altar boy, around the age of seven. Several of the older boys at school were already to be seen at Mass moving around the altar and heard exchanging Latin sentences with the priest. I assume that the suggestion for me to join this special group came from the Headmistress to my parents who would have seen the invitation as an honour. Now some of us younger boys began to learn the Latin responses and the activities of the Mass with their attendant tasks of carrying books, fetching water and wine, ringing bells and the like. A few of us continued, many until late adolescence. I quite quickly progressed to serving Mass with one established server and within a year or so I was doing so on my own at 7.30 or 8.00 a.m. in the Cathedral.

I preferred to serve Low Mass and not just because it was shorter (rarely over half an hour), or because I could be a little late for school with impunity. I had a sense of being integral to the action of the Mass, as one of a team; at that time I could not identify this notion, but there was indeed a working partnership between priest and server, and I derived pride and pleasure from being a dependable partner. I liked the Latin, as I grew increasingly accustomed to it and could remember rather than read the responses, so that eventually I was able to say them by heart and carry out my tasks by recognising what actions were associated with the Latin said by the priest. But I was a young laddie, and early rising, hasty dressing without anything to eat or drink, a brisk walk or even run to the Cathedral, (itself often freezing) could be unpleasant. To balance these factors there was always the sense of having been singled out to do something special and being viewed favourably as a result by family, family friends and teachers.

I now find myself persuaded that even then I was experiencing, without conscious realisation, a particular sense of intimacy and community; when much older I was aware of experiencing this sense in religious worship, but it must have taken root when I was around eight. Family life was intimate and school was a definite community, but participation in religious services meant routinely sharing in a common activity, with adults, children, family members, friends, people I recognised and strangers. Moreover, within that community, met in church, there was the group of people with whom, as an altar boy, I was most closely and frequently in contact, apart from my fellow servers, namely, the priests of the Cathedral and diocese. The altar boys found the priests, almost without exception, friendly and forgiving of error. I soon took it for granted that the priest would greet me with a smile and would thank me for my help in putting on his vestments; after Mass he might chat, perhaps ask about my family; he thanked me again. Some were chattier, some more pious than others. Some inspired awe, some seemed very young. We, the altar boys, had our personal favourites among these varied men, but I don't remember that we actually disliked any of the priests who staffed the Cathedral and whom we saw frequently, or any of the diocesan priests who appeared for ordinations and special Masses.

What I picked up even as a young boy was the ordinariness and the individuality of these men, who laughed, talked and smoked just like our fathers, brothers and uncles. They came largely from the North-East, and several used the Doric with each other or with some parishioners. (At a much later stage, I discovered that the vast majority liked a dram, and some an excess of drams; also, a whisper or two carried to me about a housekeeper possibly carrying out duties not sanctioned by the Church; but at no time did I hear of an unfortunate interest in boys.) In their ordinariness they provided models normally provided by adult males in the family, now too often absent; and their being linked with my religion was an advantage. I rarely meet any of these men, and indeed few survive, but I am always pleased to hear about them and feel sad when I hear that one has died.

Virtually all my memories of early family life are located in one home only, 178 Skene Street West, top flat; the Gordons lived in the middle and the Pauls on the ground floor. The house faced the Grammar School and was the last house on Skene Street West. A lane – Thistle Lane – separated us from our neighbours on the west, the door to the building was at the side of the house, and was followed closely by another door leading to the back yard. There were no houses directly opposite us, apart from the school janitor's house. A short distance west, the houses began on the opposite side, large, imposing and detached for the most part. Skene Street West occupied one block west of Rose Street, one block east of which there began a row of slum houses. I passed these poor homes daily from the age of eleven on my route between home and Gordon's College, but it was only much later, as a temporary postman during the University Christmas holiday, that I first entered them, to encounter fully the miserable sights and smells that had been hinted at on my schoolboy journeys.

The western part of Skene Street and Skene Street West were largely occupied by working and lower middle class families, a mixture of skilled workmen and tradesmen, like my father, clerks, teachers, shop assistants and managers, local civil servants, insurance agents and the like. We occupied an intermediate position physically and socio-economically between the better off, even wealthy, residents of Carden Place, Victoria Street and Albert Street and the slum-dwellers of Skene Street. And yet all three areas produced lads and lasses o' pairts, distinguishable by the school uniforms that marked an older child as a pupil at a senior secondary school.

We moved to 178 Skene Street West in 1940, as part of a three-way house exchange. (House was the word we used to describe where we lived, but in fact our area consisted almost entirely of three-storey tenements, and we lived in flats.) I have very little recollection of how all this was arranged. I seem to remember my Uncle Bill, my mother's brother, helping to move furniture, and even using (illicitly) for this purpose the van he drove as an engineer in the Post Office; my father and my other two uncles on my mother's side were all in the Army and therefore unavailable. Now our front windows looked on to the sparkling silver-grey granite facade of the Grammar School whereas from 24 Whitehall Place, our previous flat, we had only a view of the back of the school and a wide expanse of grass. The front lawns and trees provided a pastoral view, not seriously challenged by the various evening and weekend activities of the Home Guard on which the black statue of Lord Byron looked amusedly. We children compared their military activities unfavourably with those of our fathers, uncles and brothers in the armed forces, but also sensed that their activities had a serious basis. I remember best the loud commands, echoing round the green spaces, of drill sergeants, addressed to men of serious feature and obvious determination, some in civilian, others military, dress, and yet others in a mixture of the two. I could see them from our front room window on the top floor of 178 and I could hear them, from the adjoining bedroom as I lay in bed, calling out their goodnights in the male voices that were absent from my family and school life, and from that of many of my playmates; their footsteps and the clanking and swishing of bicycles occupied a minute or so, faded and then left the late evening silent.

Silence often occurred at home, in a natural way, and especially in the evening. The noises that entered the flat from outside were those of pedestrians and the occasional motor vehicle (given petrol rationing and the relative paucity of cars over fifty years ago). Our walls were thick, our floor solid, so that neighbours' lives provided very little audible evidence. Children's shouts were more easy to discern, but in the darker months of the year, or in rainy weather at any time, our family lived in an enveloping domestic and familiar atmosphere that was relatively muted, and not oppressively so. My mother's time was spent largely in the kitchen/sitting room, the focal point of all tenement life and much of ours was too, especially in the colder times of the year, for the lighting of one fire, in the black and polished range, was all that a family could normally afford. In this room my two sisters and I did our homework, or read our comics or a book; we did the same jigsaws repeatedly, we played simple card games or Ludo or Snakes and Ladders; we played with our toys, though my recollection is that noisier games – I had a fort, a toy cannon that fired matches, some toy soldiers and spent shotgun cartridges – were usually confined to the front room or the bedroom. Here we also washed and got ready for bed, with no serious issues of modesty that I can recall.

We had visitors but not often, if my remembered pleasure or even excitement at opening the door to a knock or a ring at the outside doorbell is a reliable indicator. These visitors were mainly family, and their visits were often unexpected. There was no tradition of writing to announce a forthcoming visit, nor did we (with the majority of our fellow citizens) have a telephone, and dropping by was the norm. Further, despite the restrictions imposed by wartime rationing, people had meals with us; Aunt Bella, who worked nearby, came regularly for lunch, though doubtless with some arrangements regarding food coupons, and perhaps other family members came for meals on a prearranged basis. Occasionally an old friend of my mother's from her working days would greet me when I entered the house after school, and this was always a treat, for there would be a home-baked cake or a shop-bought scone or pancake with home-made jam still on the table, usually on a three-tiered cake stand used for special occasions. Even better, there was still teatime to look forward to, for 'afternoon tea', of the scone and cake persuasion, was nothing to do with 'tea', a meal of some substance. Cheese, eggs, tinned fish (salmon a not too common but eagerly anticipated delight), bacon, sausages, salad (lettuce and tomatoes almost completely), potatoes all appeared at some time or another at 'teatime', depending on the availability of types of food, the limits of rationing, and my mother's considerable skills at managing resources and at cooking.

Bread was eaten at all meals and between them. I don't remember our breakfasts apart from cream of wheat and porridge, the latter mainly for my father. We drank milk and tea. I don't think I tasted coffee until I went to weddings in hotels, and then I didn't like it. I did taste Camp Coffee at home or at relations' houses, a liquid composed of chicory and coffee, but it probably passed for exotic in the Scottish diet, further restricted by rationing. A special treat as a drink was Hay's 'lemonade'. 'Lemonade' or 'ale' was used by us generically to refer to all of Hay's products, manufactured locally and distributed in rattling arrogance by lorries or horse-drawn carts. The bottles were taller than milk bottles and through their clear glass could be seen yellow, orange, red, brown, green or transparent liquids with bubbles that hinted at the froth to come. These were kept in our house under the sink and brought out with permission (though an occasional surreptitious swig did occur) for a treat. They featured at school, church and Cub parties, accompanied by sandwiches and 'fine pieces', and were always associated with the notion of something special.

Our main meal was dinner, eaten during the school week between morning and afternoon school and at weekends and holiday times at a more flexible time. The word 'lunch' took hold in my vocabulary only after I had left secondary school, for even there it was 'school dinners' that were eaten in the middle of the day. I have often heard my aunts and uncles say that they 'didn't know how your mother managed' to feed the three of us and herself during the war, but she must have had great skill. She baked often, despite the rationing of sugar and I grew up assuming that cake was a fairly frequent feature of family meals. She said she could not make bread, and I don't think she ever tried to for us, but fresh bread was readily available from the many bakers clustered at the top end of Union Street, or even the corner shops, and I don't suppose that it occurred to me to feel deprived by my mother's not baking her own. For dinner, mince, stews and soups predominated, and stovies; meat came inevitably with potatoes, but green vegetables were less common and less appreciated by me, children in general, and the general population. We ate the stuff because 'it was good for you' but we were unconvinced. Fridays were meatless days; we ate fish, but I did so dutifully, considering it a poor substitute for meat. Macaroni and cheese was much preferred, steaming and creamy, with the baked cheese on top smelling and tasting tangy.

Then there were the puddings. How easily I recall these – hot, sweet, filling and fulfilling, rich in taste and smell. Custard figured prominently, poured over sponges or tinned fruit or on its own, as did fruit pies – apple, which I disliked, or rhubarb, which I liked when sweetened; to this day I love the mixed textures of fruit and pastry in a baked pie. Fruit I ate but tended not to seek – rationing made it a treat, but it could not compete with pudding. Dessert was of course the high point of dinner, the motivation when needed to finish off vegetables; second helpings were often available, perhaps at the expense of my parents' share, but no such thought occurred to me then.

Images come to me of my home in flashes rather than sequences. Again, light plays a part, this time the artificial light of an evening or late afternoon in winter, yielded by gas mantles, glowing yellow or white, for we had no electricity. Yet 'glowing' does not capture the ceaseless work of the mantle, which had the semblance of living and effort-making. The light shone brightly but seemed to tremble; the shadows it cast were not the fixed silhouettes yielded by electric light but were as if some form of life that attempted to keep still but could not quite succeed. In the late afternoon, before the gas went on, the red glow of the fire in the range inset in the kitchen wall comforted the room, and us, until the preparations for teatime began; these included ensuring the fire had a red glow, against which we toasted bread extended on a four-pronged fork made of wire just sufficiently long for us to tolerate the heat. We toasted one side only and for years I compared unfavourably the toast encountered at wedding receptions in hotels or in (rarely visited) cafes with what I knew to be real toast – hot from the fire, toasted on one side and showing the patterns of the grill which was at the front of our kitchen fire.

The auditory images I have tend to blend in with the many more and clearer visual ones, as in the case of the pulsating, hissing gas mantle. But one stands out on its own. The other sound occupied more the foreground, though at times it shared our attention with other activities of a quiet nature such as drawing or ironing or sewing. This was the radio. I don't know how often it was on, but as it required, in a non-electrical household, two batteries, one wet and the other dry, it would obviously not be switched on indiscriminately. The news was of major importance, but I think that my mother, or parents when my father was home on leave, probably listened to it more when we children were in bed or out at school or play. Nevertheless I can remember the news broadcast being introduced and ending with, 'and this is John Snagge/Alvar Liddell… reading it'. The full import of what was said was beyond me, beyond the general sense that 'we' had won a battle or campaign or that things looked bad in Africa or Russia or at sea.

The war was, however, dealt with differently in variety shows and comedy series. In the former, such as Workers' Playtime, jokes about the enemy were greeted with applause and cheers; of the latter it is ITMA (It's That Man Again) that I remember, 'that man' being Tommy Handley, assisted by the impressionist, Jack Train, and others, who created a group of comic characters, especially Funf, the incompetent and always thwarted spy. My later appreciation of the Goon Show was grounded, I think, in this first comedy series that I remember. Then there was light music (not to my taste), Scottish country dance music (better, but not a real choice), and big band swing (much better); unfortunately my mother did not like the latter. I don't think I heard jazz then but swing certainly prepared the way for a later love of jazz, through such bands as that of Joe Loss. Radio, however, did not dominate – it was switched on for a purpose, and switched off when a programme was finished. It punctuated our life and no more.

I recall family life being lived with a quiet intensity and completeness – things were as they were and alternative views, of things as they might be, did not seriously occupy me. There were, of course, 'I wish/hope that…' elements in my life, ranging from '…that I could get a lot of toy soldiers for Christmas' to '…that Daddy was coming home soon'. The former sort of desire was episodic and keenly felt but, when ending in disappointment, fairly easily disposed of. The second somehow became part of the fabric of my life, ever-present but not dominant, only occasionally becoming sharp. I realised that the world was created and organised in ways beyond my control, for at every turn we were told that there were no sweets, bananas, real ice-cream, street lighting, travel, or paper to write on in school because 'there's a war on'. Our fathers, uncles, brothers and even aunts and cousins could not be with us because 'they're away in the Army/Navy/Air Force'. These deprivations tended not to obsess us on a moment-by-moment basis; paradoxically they became most clear when one was challenged or temporarily removed, by the arrival in shops of a consignment of sweets or fruit or in the breaking of the blackout restriction when a blind fell down, leading to a household panic and shouts from outside the offending home of 'Put that light out'. The most important deprivation was known as such when my father came home, stayed briefly, and left; the gap in our family became clear and then slowly became less apparent.

Our family experienced no deaths or casualties and so we never felt the direct impact of searing and irreplaceable personal loss. Doubtless my parents knew families where a father or son was killed or wounded; and for most of the war my mother had the ceaseless anxiety of my father's, and two uncles' (her brother and brother-in-law), being abroad, with only intermittent letters arriving and always the dread that one of these would be formal and final, in a nondescript official envelope. Thus, my deprivations never became tragic; they constituted aspects of the world-as-it-was and were accepted automatically and not articulated. Nevertheless, for most of the population, wartime was a time of fear and unnatural limitations; the second we children heard about constantly, and the first we sensed, from adults. I suppose I began to realise some of these attitudes for myself as the war gradually turned in favour of the Allies, and phrases such as 'when the war is over…', 'once your father comes back' became more frequent. Yet, while we talked about sweets being plentiful and unrationed, about what a banana really tasted like, about not blacking out our windows, about seeing our fathers, brothers etc. again, that is, in terms of return to old experiences, we were actually dealing with the creation of new ones. I had been six at the outbreak of war, and four years had dimmed, distorted or obliterated the past. Thus I, like many others of my age, was puzzled and felt let down when, at the end of the war, life did not bring continuous dramatic changes.

While the war shaped and conditioned all our lives at a profound level, for a young boy it inevitably offered material for games and drawings and stories, in all of which the Germans came off worse. I devoured an illustrated book called *The First Year of the War in Pictures*, finding in it the visual referents, in photographs and paintings by war artists, for the words that I heard on the radio or saw in the *Evening Express*, the *Sunday Post* and, more rarely, the *Press and Journal*. I drew aerial dogfights at school and at home, and naval and tank battles; machines were easier to draw than people, as I could copy the pictures I saw in books and comics. In the latter the drawings were few, though clear and accurate, to our knowledge, being illustrations to the heroic texts of the stories in the *Hotspur*, the *Wizard*, the *Adventure*, and the *Rover* (I think I have listed these in my order of preference, as there is a mantra-like quality in the recitation). In games nobody minded being a German because being shot or blown up invited a dramatic display of staggering and collapsing, accompanied by blood-curdling cries. Our physical or verbal or drawn representations of warfare and the reality of death and destruction shown in photographs or cinema newsreels inhabited different universes. To some extent this was due to what must have been a conspiracy of silence among the adults who dealt with us; while we heard that people had died, servicemen or civilians, and often in huge numbers, the monstrous details were not passed on to us. They were talked about in our playground or neighbourhood conversations, but at the same level of accuracy as our talk of sex. And then we, as a family, were lucky not to be bombed, despite Aberdeen's being one of the most consistently attacked cities in Scotland and proportionately heavily bombed. I do not remember having a personal sense of danger throughout the war, and that must have been as a result of the adults', especially my mother's, shielding us. Going around the city with my mother, to visit or to a place of interest, we came across burned out buildings, but our familiar and local areas and Union Street, where we sometimes went to the pictures or shopping, went virtually unscathed. Thus we were spared direct confrontation with attacks on people and property, even though we knew from the gunfire and frantic stabbing of searchlights that a raid was going on and heard the next day of the casualties. Indeed, I remember looking down from the top deck of a tramcar, as it slowly lurched round the corner from Union Terrace to Rosemount Viaduct, on to crowds outside the Public Library attempting to read the casualty lists pinned up on boards.

The centre of Aberdeen was a ceaseless reminder of wartime, for it was filled with Allied troops, especially sailors, given Aberdeen's status as a port. I remember seeing Dutch, Norwegian, French, Danish, Belgian, Russian, Canadian, American, Indian, South African, New Zealand and Australian sailors and their counterparts in the army, together with Poles and Czechs and doubtless others. Airmen were from fewer countries, but were the most glamorous of our allies, in that they fought in the skies above us, taking off from airfields in the North-East. Outside Aberdeen there were three big camps for the Polish Army, who not surprisingly tended to predominate in the city. Their reputation was mixed: they were said to be ferocious fighters, but prone to moods and depression. (A former Polish medical officer told me years later that there was a high rate of suicide in these camps.) They were too, in the euphemism we heard in fascinated ignorance, 'ladies' men', and certainly they seemed to us children to be fond of brilliantining their hair and wearing it longer than our troops. We heard of mutterings among British troops about these glamorous foreigners enchanting – and more – the local women, and of fights in pubs and on the street. Many, however, settled in the North-East, marrying and raising families. My major memory of them is their filing into the right hand aisle of St Mary's Cathedral for Sunday morning High Mass and singing in a powerful and moving way I had not heard before, with a tone that came back to me when I first encountered the term 'Slav melancholy'.

In the Cathedral on Sunday morning, at all Masses, but especially the eleven o'clock High Mass, the drabness of wartime civilian dress was offset by the uniforms of all nations. I think I realised something of the enormity of the disruption that had brought these men to us. In the congregation too sat small groups of Italian and German prisoners-of-war in sloppy uniforms with distinctive patches; this was not to the taste of everyone, especially those with loved ones serving abroad or prisoners of war, and even more so those who had lost a husband, son or brother. These prisoners typically worked on local farms, replacing farm workers in the services, and we considered them 'good' Germans and Italians, glad to be out of the war, farmers and farm workers themselves. Whatever the truth of that, they were to be found on Union Street, as well as in the Cathedral on Sunday morning, usually without escort, especially as the war went on. As children, we did not fear them. I don't think that we feared any troops; we were always in at night, or usually accompanied if out, because of the blackout, and during the day we, and they, found of greatest interest the busiest and thus safest parts of the City – Union Street, George Street, Market Street, and the Castlegate.

My father had joined the Territorial Army in the 1920s, and was therefore called up rapidly at the outbreak of war. He did not go overseas until 1942 and returned just after the war ended. We saw him off occasionally at the Joint Station (the shell near the entrance today brings it back) but neither of my parents liked a public parting; more often he left 178 to walk in his brisk way to the station. How often I cried I cannot say, for I remember only one episode; looking down from our front room I saw him in his khaki uniform, rifle and pack, not turning back, striding away and I wept bitterly. My mother came through and comforted me and all was well. I don't know if I had, or stated, a fear that he might not come back, or whether this was his leaving to go abroad, but the bitter grief comes back to me still.

My young boy's memory struggled to remember the details of his face, his appearance, his voice, and his smell at the end of a working day, a composite of sweat, tobacco and the indefinable traces of wire, tools, and insulating tape that he used as an electrical engineer. I have photographs of him on leave in Rome, a wonderful experience for someone to whom Rome, St Peter's and the Vatican must in ordinary circumstances have seemed impossibly remote. We were excited to receive his letters and photographs; we wrote to him and sent drawings; at night we prayed for him, as also for Uncle Bill and Uncle Ivor, in the Royal Artillery and the Royal Army Medical Corps respectively, and also in the African and Italian campaigns. Recognisably our father, from the tone of his letters, my mother's reaction to them and his photographs, he was also associated with the exotic – foreign lands, cities almost of myth, hot climates, palm trees, camels and so on. His rank as staff-sergeant entitled him to a revolver, and he once allowed my sisters and me to handle it; I doubt if he could ever have fired it in combat, or the rifle I sometimes saw him carrying as he left us to go back to camp. Fortunately he was not put to the test, or, if he was, I heard nothing of it, for he spoke rarely of the war and his participation in it, a characteristic shared by my uncles, who, if not combat soldiers, were close to the field of action when a battle was under way.

Our family lived a self-contained life but not an isolated one. We lived in a tenement building housing two other families, at the end of a row of tenements; virtually everybody walked – to school, to work, or to the shops; we tended to shop within a reasonably close distance at a narrow range of shops. Thus we saw the same people all the time, on the way to and from destinations or play, in shops, both behind and in front of the counter, as well as in church or in school. Mr Bruce, the Rose Street butcher, and his assistants recognised my sisters and me if any of us went to his shop; in the absence of my father, he signed a letter in support of my application for Robert Gordon's College, where his son had already been a pupil. The staff in the Co-op in Huntly Street took the shopping list my mother had written, filled it and gave the correct change from the closely calculated sum of money I handed over. Adults smiled or said hello frequently as we passed each other almost daily, en route to school and work. I would often call for some friend at his house, or be called for, and so knew by name and face a wide range of parents, mainly mothers, given the absence of fathers in the services.

The adults whom we knew best were our relations, for our visitors were primarily our aunts and uncles. On my mother's side, the Smiths, Aunt Bella was the most frequent visitor, as she worked in an office within ten minutes' walk, and usually ate with us at midday. Her husband, Uncle Bill, was in the Royal Artillery, and visited on leave. In insurance before the war, he had a small car in which we were taken for runs out to the country, a special event. I have an image of sitting between his knees in the driving seat holding the steering wheel, and seeing his nicotine-stained fingers beside my uninteresting pale ones. Aunt Muriel came by too, also working in a government office, latterly with Uncle Cameron, not in the Army but a Bevin boy, whose heart condition led to a far too early death. Uncle Ivor, the youngest of my mother's family and seventeen years her junior, I saw as dashing before and in the early part of the war; he had been to Gordon's College and his example was put before me by his sisters. My mother's other brother, Uncle Bill, referred to as Brother Bill by his sisters to distinguish him from Aunt Bella's husband, was in a reserved occupation in the Post Office. He helped my mother out in my father's absence, in moving and repair work and dropped in and out at various times, having the use of a van.

My father was the third youngest of eight Davidsons and many of his elder brothers and sisters had families, so that I knew several cousins. We visited the Davidson relations; Aunt Ruth, my father's eldest sister, and Uncle Jake shared a tenement flat in Stafford Street with my cousins Ruth and Mary, and Aunt Amy. Uncle Harry and Aunt Bella, in a Fraser Street tenement, had two boys and two girls, the former being close in age to my sisters and me. I don't remember the adult conversations but there would doubtless be questions about the war and about who had heard most recently from Eddie, Norrie, Charlie and Mary, my father's brothers and sister in Canada and the USA.

When visitors came to 178, the kettle went on, the table was spread and bread and jam, biscuits, or cake would appear. I cannot remember my grandmother, Grammie, visiting, though I think Grandpa did so, but not often: they were my mother's parents, my only grandparents, the Davidsons having died before my father was married. They lived about ten minutes' walk away, and we as a family often saw them. At one point during the war my mother was ill and my sisters and I stayed with them. Grammie was our focus, bustling and couthie, who made the same sort of hearty food as my mother, and fussed somewhat. Grandpa was kindly but stayed in the background, doing nothing in the house, sitting by the fire smoking a pungent pipe after his tea, at the end of his day's work as a joiner in Hall's shipyard. As their family had grown up, their material circumstances had improved to the extent that they had a traditional 'front room', rarely used, and holding a display cabinet with china and ornaments; above all it contained a piano, on which I occasionally laid a finger, without musical success or encouragement from my grandparents.

Neighbours were less often in our home, but I don't remember any of them at our table, and it may have been for the neighbourly reason that no one wished to strain the meagre resources of another household. But one group of people did appear before my father went abroad, his fellow soldiers. On several occasions I came home from school to find one strange soldier, or even two, with my parents and then our all sitting down to tea. The circumstances I don't know; at some times my father was stationed locally or within a reasonable distance and offered his hospitality to a fellow staff-sergeant. Perhaps these visits were always preceded by a letter, perhaps only sometimes. The pattern continued for me as a University student, when I brought friends home at different times, always to be met with a snack or a meal.

Without doubt the grandest occasions in our family life were weddings, typically the culmination of fairly lengthy engagements, and prepared for carefully. The phrase 'bottom drawer' comes to me from my childhood; I knew that young women did buy and lay away – in drawers, chests or shelves – domestic items that would be needed when they got married. I remember forthcoming weddings being discussed within the family – mainly to do with the clothes to be worn – and especially with visitors. On the great day ordinary realities were obscured by the magical pomp of wedding dresses, suits with tails, best and colourful dresses and hats for women, and best and dark suits (or military uniforms) for the men, in a flower-decked church and exotically smelling hotel. We children had some licence, there being many adults to distract each other from their normal vigilance and we explored the world inside which we found ourselves for half a day. I remember the fascination of large rooms – dining rooms, lounges, reception rooms – and large toilets – with fitments giving off fascinating noises – with an ever-changing population of wedding guests, hotel guests and bar drinkers, and that rarest of experiences, standing at a stall in a row filled with men, while I negotiated the hazards of buttons on a new or special pair of short trousers or the holding up of a rarely worn kilt, lest disaster befall.

I remember also the strangeness of eating in a hotel, with rules to be observed that I did not grasp but knew were important, regarding a battery of cutlery, plates of impressive size and pattern and identical to those before everyone else, and waiting while others were served or finished a course. The food was different; the belief that it had to be better because hotel-made conflicted often with the evidence of my taste buds, but on offer were chicken, then a delicacy in the average home, lemonade and ice cream. Fresh fruit lacked the sweetness I enjoyed, but ice cream compensated for that. Coffee was for the adults and its exotic nature was added to by what seemed toy cups, the demi-tasses. Wedding cake I disliked; I barely managed to swallow the fragment of the dark sticky over-ripe concoction that etiquette demanded before passing the rest on to someone with incomprehensible taste; to this day I cannot eat marzipan. Speeches made little sense – at least the content did not, for I did have a sense that they were part of a ritual that adults followed and presumably understood. On the other hand, they produced laughter, and I had little experience of seeing a group of adults laughing together, outside an occasional visit to the cinema, and certainly not at a meal table and dressed in their best.

Then came the dancing. All children took part, dancing with adults and other children at the firm suggestion of an adult. I remember also musical chairs, the Grand Old Duke of York and much hilarity. By this stage, men's jackets were often off, the bar was heavily patronised, and indulgence to children at its greatest. We played, romped, drank unlimited lemonade, watched in incredulous delight our elders unbend, squabbled, got dirty and, if younger, fell asleep. Perhaps it was at this point in a wartime wedding that women missed their absent husbands most, when their children were under a communal watchful eye and they had a chance to relax and enjoy the company; certainly the occasion must have been poignant.

I was a city child, but knew well only a few areas and routes between them and my home. Going downtown meant the company of an adult, and my discovery of Union Street and its surrounds tended to take place in a context of shopping with my parents, more usually my mother, and my sisters. The countryside I hardly remember visiting at all. There were a few trips with Uncle Bill in his car, which must have ceased early in the war. I have a vague recollection of being on a pilgrimage by train to the Abbey of Old Deer, and then only an image of crowds and singing. The Cubs went on picnics to Cults, where we ate and played by the Shakkin' Briggie, then functional, well-kept and well patronised. With the Cubs I also went to Hazlehead on summer's evenings, and again my strongest image is of light, but this time associated with a sense of something beyond me. The image is of my looking at my shadow, long in the evening sun, stretching far across the grass, and almost reaching a screen of bushes, perhaps the rhododendrons which characterised that large parkland. As I look at the shadow, I am aware – despite being part of a group – of being profoundly alone, not lonely, but simply existing in my own right and not by virtue of anyone else. It was a very strong experience and remains a very vivid image.

Hazlehead was then on the edge of Aberdeen, barely fringed by houses and reached by tramcar. The tram would pursue a stately enough passage up Queen's Road, as befitted its large granite houses, but then the tramlines veered left and the tram took on a new life; it went flat out, swaying along what might have been a quarter mile of track with no stops until it came to the terminus, a rustic wooden shelter. If we were lucky, the tram had at each end of its upper deck an open area, with a curved wooden bench and iron railing, to occupy which meant a stiff breeze, an exaggerated swaying, much sliding about and a firm grip on the railings, all accompanied by shrieks of mock terror – and perhaps not always mock. Once arrived at Hazlehead, we played the usual Cowboys and Indians, British and German, goodies and baddies, or perhaps football; we did not go far, for Hazlehead seemed huge and included large tracts of trees without clear markers. But we made the most of our time there, for it represented an expedition to the edge of our known world, and returning on the tram was like leaving the country for the city.

The Westburn and Victoria parks were different from Hazlehead, much nearer – within walking distance, smaller and well defined by roads, walls and railings. The Westburn was for playing, with part of the Denburn emerging briefly from a tunnel to keep an artificial wading pool fresh before disappearing underground. Some distance away was a concrete area with swings and a chute and a sandpit. We played in both areas but also all over the park, for we could kick a ball around or re-enact goodies and baddies all over the grassy areas. We noticed, without interest, the bowling greens, patronised by elderly people but they were in their own enclosure and the park was ours. By contrast, the Victoria Park on the opposite side of the road was an adults' park, where playing about incurred the descent of the parkie, quite properly fearing for the flowers and shrubs which were the park's chief feature.

My encounters with nature were thus largely confined to the parks of Aberdeen, with trips to the beach on occasion. They didn't really count, however, as they tended to involve watching people playing on the sand, eating ice-cream after a picnic and watching boats rather than the sea. We paddled, made sand castles, looked for crabs, and got our clothes wet. Nature was, however, much more obviously a part of city life than it is now. Several farms were inside the city boundary; cattle were driven from Kittybrewster Station down Great Northern Road and George Street to the slaughterhouse on Hutcheon Street, and I have still an image of frightened beasts, lowing and rolling their eyes, as they were herded round the last corner to the grim and smelly building. Petrol rationing forced vans and trucks off the road, to be replaced by horse-drawn carts. The horses were huge, to my upward-turned gaze, and magnificent, with great legs stockinged below the knee in long hair. Their hooves clattered, and on the cassies which covered many streets the hooves seemed to echo, besides giving off sparks. Their smell was powerful but not unpleasant, once the initial whiff of sharn had been absorbed. Occasionally a driver would let us pat his horse, or even feed it some hay or a carrot and I remember the awe with which I saw very near to my outstretched hand the huge yellow teeth suddenly revealed as the upper lip was raised.

On cold days the steam rose from these patient beasts, and the breath jetted from their nostrils in what seemed a larger, more powerful version of the cigarette smoke expelled nasally by talented smokers. Steam also rose from the – again to my eyes – monumental tumuli of turds that marked a horse's route, and from the oily, yellow urine that ran down the gutters into branders which seemed to have an endless appetite for such things. We eventually took for granted the evidence of a horse's recent presence, but considered ourselves blessed with good fortune if we were actually witness to the processes of expulsion, which seemed to go on for ever and without effort. Real fascination, however, was reserved for the sight of a horse with an erection, the purpose of which we only vaguely understood but the importance of which was undoubted, from its size and rigidity and the attention it attracted (or studiously did not) from passers-by. The sight was not a frequent one, and I was privileged in this way on perhaps only a handful of occasions, but each sighting yielded considerable material for discussion and speculation among my male friends.

My only full exposure to country life occurred in the summer of 1940 or 1941, when my father was stationed in Fife, near Burntisland, and was billeted with a farmer's family with whom we spent a fortnight. I discovered teenagers who could, and did, use a shotgun, herds of cows in fields and in the milking shed, hens strutting their superiority in the farmyard or even inside the farmhouse, rabbits in unseemly numbers, and the joys of jumping on to bales of hay and straw from rafters. Despite these novel and often rewarding experiences (my collection of empty cartridges used as toy soldiers was formed here), I was and remained a city child, for going to the shops in Burntisland to buy comics and cardboard aeroplanes to fire from a simple catapult offered equal pleasure. I absorbed the fact that the children who lived on the farm had a different way of life, different knowledge and different attitudes; I think that to some extent their assuredness in their way of life was intimidating, but I was not with them for long enough to have to adapt to, or even adopt, anything different. And a day or two back in familiar haunts and ways was enough to remove any confusion and restore me to my unambiguous status as a city child.

In writing autobiographically I make no claim to importance for myself, but only that memories of one childhood may illuminate, if only partially and fitfully, some aspects of the cultural contexts in which it was lived. I have attempted to reconstruct my inscape of over half a century ago as a means of identifying aspects of the landscape within which it grew and had its being. As my focus has been on my perceptions, then and now, I have not attended to chronology nor to 'historical' facts (some details may well not accord fully with actual verifiable events). Nor have I attempted to present a full account of family events and membership, friends and schooling. What I have presented emerged as I thought and wrote. (Richard Hoggart said well of writing autobiographically that 'your mind is like a magnet you own but do not control, and all the memories iron filings.') Both ordering and significance naturally occurred, but selection of detail was required if the chapter were not to become a book.

Though many themes occurred to me as I wrote, I did not attempt to work through any of them in analytic mode, seeing that as inappropriate. Yet I realised during the writing that I was in fact creating a record of the growth of awareness and its concomitant loss of innocence, whatever the aspect of landscape I was describing. And, at the end of my task, I find distance has not lent enchantment to my childhood but it has encouraged further that growth of awareness.

Memories of a Calvinist Childhood

David Hay

Innocence

I cannot recall being critical of my father until I was in my thirteenth year. Even then I was unwilling to believe my senses. It was 1948 and the two of us were standing outside the arched Victorian doorway of the boarding house of Queen Elizabeth's School, a small country Grammar School in Crediton in South West England. I was, suddenly, about to become a pupil there after a childhood spent in North East Scotland, mostly in the village of Rhynie in Strathbogie. My father rang the bell. A middle-aged secretary came to the door, escorted my trunk into the hallway and asked my father if he would like to come in with me for a few minutes. No, that would not be necessary.

So I was alone in an alien land. Now, in middle age, I realise that my father was a shy man, uneasy with schools and officialdom, but then I felt bereft. They put me in a dormitory with twenty or so other boys who couldn't understand my accent, not very surprising because even Aberdonians had laughed at my uncouth Strathbogie dialect. The struggle for a 'kintra chiel fae Rhynie' was to appear polished amongst the English, the very people that I saw as the arbiters of sophistication, and I knew that the best I could do would be a fake.

My salvation was an addiction to 'Smith of the Lower Third' a serial in the *Wizard*, one of D C Thomson's many efforts for the young. Smith was a working class boy who, via the implementation of recommendations of the Fleming Report, had been sent to school among the toffs. His experiences of coping with posh manners, unpleasant school traditions, T A K Simmerson the school bully and A P E Carew the school hero, provided a template for my behaviour and when I suffered, solace, because Smith was suffering too.

In the end, you learn a culture or go under, and I learned how to be an

Englishman, even to the extent of becoming head of the Boarding House I had entered so unwillingly. I went back home to university in Aberdeen in 1954, a foreigner yet again. Sexually and in terms of the politics of emotion I was extremely naïve, but I had some severe notions in my head about the seriousness of life, about the complexity and difficulty of understanding other people and an intensity about religion which haunts me to this day. It did not feel like innocence: more like raw, embarrassed bewilderment.

When was life innocent? Certainly at the beginning. My father, John Hay, was a merchant seaman who had come ashore when his only son was expected and got himself a job as an insurance agent. The choice of venue was either of the remote villages of Rhynie or Clatt in West Aberdeenshire. He selected the larger centre, astride the road from Alford to Huntly and at the foot of the pass that leads over the Cabrach to Dufftown and the Spey Valley. My mother, Bella Lumsden, had been an upholstress with Galloway and Sykes on Union Street in Aberdeen. I fancy she saw herself as a cut above the generality in Rhynie. She held the opinion that I had spoken very nicely until I went to school, but from then on my accent had become 'coorse'.

The rendering of 'coorse' as 'coarse' in standard English does not represent fully the sense of evil that hovers round the word. 'Coorse chiels' in Rhynie were hard men who disappeared for days on end, reputedly to spend their time downing whisky in the Grouse Inn in the Cabrach. The Cabrach was synonymous with the wilds. Crofters living up there got snowed in for the winter and there were stories, how true I do not know, of shepherds freezing to death. The only character I ever consciously encountered from there was 'Bee Wullie', who apart from keeping bees was also a mole catcher. He used to come and set gin traps on our lawn from time to time at my mother's request.

Once in a while tinkers descended on Rhynie down the Cabrach road, having presumably come over from Speyside. They sold clothes pegs at the door and sometimes one of them would play the bagpipes in the square, busking for money. My impression was that the Rhynie people despised them: the worst condemnation that could be (and was) made of certain people in the village was that they were 'jist coorse tinks'. Nice people steered clear of them and my mother definitely considered herself in that category. Hence by *fiat*, I too was meant to be nice.

This implied a number of pre-requisites, most of them covered by a Presbyterian upbringing. I had to know the Bible. My earliest memory of being literate is of sitting at home reading some Old Testament story to my mother. Perhaps it was Samuel's selection of the boy David to be God's anointed. The account tickled my infant vanity since a hero with the same name as me, 'ruddy, and withal of a beautiful countenance, and goodly to look at' came out of obscurity to win a kingdom. I remember very few stories from my early childhood other than those drawn from the Bible. Whether this was due to the direction of my mother or because of personal predilection, I cannot say.

My memories of childhood religion, in so far as I can retrieve them, are entirely benevolent. The most positive image is of an old man in a black suit and clerical collar, sitting in his garden sunning himself. We children used to cadge silver threepenny bits from him, and he always delivered the goods. Mr McHardy was the retired minister of Rhynie parish church. He had a certain amount of glamour for me because he came from Tomintoul, a village high in the 'real' Highlands beyond Strathdon. But he was also the cause of amusement because of his absent mindedness. His occasional spells of standing in for the incumbent minister tended towards chaos as he struggled to maintain a linear sequence to our worship. Whenever I think of him, I think of religion as good.

Respect for religion did not necessarily extend to all its functionaries. An elderly former missionary living in the village, nicknamed China Johnny, used to wander the roads talking to himself. Children used to lie in wait for him, hidden behind a drystone dyke, and as he passed shout 'Look at the mannie speakin' till himsel'. It never failed. He would stop, whirl round in fury and bellow at the top of his voice 'A prophet is not without honour, save in his own country!' We knew of course the source of his text, and the country in which his mind rambled.

A parallel curious phenomenon associated with early scriptural reading was my tendency to conflate the geography of our region with that of the Bible. The most dominant physical feature in the Rhynie area is the bulk of the Tap o'Noth, which I always had in mind in church when the minister told us about Mount Sinai. My vision was of Moses stumbling down through the heather on the Tap with the Tablets of the Law, on his way to deliver them to the recalcitrant people of Rhynie. These early images don't dissolve easily and I noticed on a recent climb to the top that my associations with the hill are still to do with sacredness. Similarly, on a warm summer evening towards the gloaming, the road from Rhynie to Gartly continues to evoke intensely numinous images of the meeting of Jesus with the two disciples on the road to Emmaus.

Sundays, though not vivid, were not as drab as the stereotype requires: nor were they as strict as was the rule in the West Highlands. On the whole shoes were cleaned, Sunday best laid out and food prepared on Saturday evening to minimise servile work on the following day. Church was an obligation that I never questioned and, in accord with tradition, to keep me quiet during the sermon my mother gave me a pandrop to suck. She was relatively relaxed about entertainment on the Sabbath though it was hardly outrageous. For example, we often took a walk to the cemetery which in Rhynie, in the Highland fashion, lies outside the village. The overt purpose of these outings, I assume, was to meditate on life's brief span, a thought that often returns to mind in this, my mid-passage through life. Covertly, my entertainment was to search for what I believed to be the oldest stones near the back wall of the cemetery, because they were decorated with skulls and cross bones which seemed very gruesome and reminded me of pirates. I didn't realise that a couple of stones with strange carvings on them, dumped at the gate[1], were very much older remains of our Pictish forebears.

My father was not part of this Presbyterian formality, but it is of him that I have my earliest memories. He kept hens in the field across the road from our house on the Bogie Road. I remember helping him to carry food across the road to the hens, though I suppose really I must have been hanging on to the bucket for support. I was probably about two years' old. While he was seeing to some task or other he put me in a henhouse, full of day old chicks. I rather enjoyed it, though it was through the chickens that I first became aware of death. One or two of them, instead of cheeping loudly, simply stood there with their eyes shut. 'They're shargers', my father would say. 'I'll be getting rid of them'. He had a book about sexing chicks, with photographs showing how to do the job.

[1] At the time of writing they have been placed under cover near the cemetery entrance

It looked as if you had to squeeze their insides out and it made me feel sick because I got the idea that the process killed them. I hadn't connected up the fact that the chicks were supposed to grow into adult egg layers to support the family budget.

The other early memory of my father was of him sitting me on his knee in the kitchen and feeding me soup out of a bowl. I think my mother must have been away in Aberdeen, otherwise she would not have put up with such sloppy behaviour. I knew that I should have been in my high chair and felt that this was the behaviour of an amateur.

Nevertheless I loved the relaxed feeling, for that was how my father was when he was young and strong.

Looking back, the first inklings of expulsion from Eden were when I went to school. I began my formal education with Miss Martin in Rhynie school at the age of four. There were three classes under her supervision, set in parallel rows down the room. We began with slate pencils and slates in the row seated to her left and looked enviously over to where the next class was writing with pencils in exercise books, then beyond to the Himalayas of the writer's art, where the literary set in Class Three were dipping their pens in inkwells 'Come ye blessed of my Father and sit on my right.'

My mother had taught me to read and write before I arrived at school and as a result I quickly became Dux of my class and stayed there. She had required of me that when I spoke I 'put on the English'. 'Speaking English', was a skill much needed by Rhynie people for purposes of comprehensibility when communicating with outsiders. The difficulty for me was the fact that I had arrived in school with an English (i.e. city of Aberdeen) intonation, and it led to me being labelled a cissy. In addition, my mother's views on the appropriate clothing for children did not always coincide with the requirements of Rhynie fashion, which went in for the slow and rugged look.

I soon got rid of my city accent and acquired the Doric, but my mother would permit only a limited number of tackets on my boots. Rhynie loons wore tackety boots with a vengeance: it was a case of the more tackets the better. Arbiters of high style would sit on the school steps comparing the shining rows of metal studs on the soles of their boots before running round the playground striking fire and thunder off the surface. Running fast was thought soft. You had to do a slow lumber like a cart horse, with the result that the cissies tended to win the races laid on by the teachers, making themselves still more unpopular with the fashionable set.

My mother used to make most of my clothes, including my shirts. She felt, I think, that there was something not quite proper about braces, or gallases (I never knew as a child that the word was 'gallowses'). For this reason my braces were concealed under my shirt which had, near the waistline, a set of six little slots edged with buttonhole stich, through which poked the leather tabs so that they could be lodged safely on the appropriate buttons on my trousers. There was a further complication in winter. If I was not wearing combinations, which I hated, I wore woollen underpants which had strips of tape at the top, under which could be slipped the tabs of my braces, as a means of preventing the underpants concertina-ing in a heap down my legs. This latter device was not considered cissy, because it resembled the system operating on the long johns worn by the older men in the village. Another fashion item was the helmet, which vied with the balaclava as the appropriate protection in winter. The idea was to try to get one that looked as much like a pilot's leather flying helmet as possible. Again, I never really made it in those stakes, having to make do with a rather weedy peaked affair.

Shopping in Rhynie when you were a kid was very limited. The two items I remember purchasing were lucky bags and Japanese paper flowers. Lucky bags could be bought for a few pence from one of the shops in the main street. You never knew what was in the bags and simply took pot luck: I think they were made up by the shopkeeper to tempt us kids, and as far as I remember, never contained anything worth having. Japanese paper flowers were something else. You bought a bivalve shell and took it home and put it in a jar of water. After a while the shell would open and a brightly coloured paper flower would emerge and spread up through the water. I thought they were amazing and bought quite a few of them.

By the time my education was under way, Scotland was at war. I suppose this might have signalled a further curtailment of innocence, but it didn't. My father's background in the merchant service meant that when the war broke out he volunteered and became an officer on a rescue ship accompanying the North Atlantic convoys. After assembling in Scapa

Flow on this side of the Atlantic, the convoy made its way to Halifax in Nova Scotia, picked up supplies and returned to a beleaguered homeland. My father's task was to command a rescue launch, picking up people left alive after the inevitable U-Boat attacks, and of course leaving himself and his crew very vulnerable in the process. Readers of Montserrat's *The Cruel Sea* will be aware of the terror and misery of those convoys, but my consciousness contained nothing of that. By this stage my father was a good looking stranger in uniform who came home occasionally, bringing gifts from Canada, chocolate, which I had never seen, a pair of skis that I never used, and toys. I was very impressed by his naval uniform and felt superior to those kids, most of them, whose parents were farmers or farm labourers. I did not know I was of peasant stock myself.

The most conspicuous evidence of war in Rhynie was the criss crosses of sticky paper across the classroom windows to protect us from bomb blast. We also had to carry our gas masks to school in cardboard boxes slung over our shoulders. Gas masks were fun, because you could make farting noises with them as you slid them over your face and people's voices sounded weirdly claustrophobic inside them. At home, my mother had fixed up a table with an old mattress on top of it for us to huddle under in the event of a bomber attack. Nazi plans for the annihilation of Rhynie did not get beyond the drawing board stage. As far as I am aware we never saw even a single enemy plane though I remember someone claiming that Hitler had, deservedly, dropped a bomb on the Cabrach.

One day a whole stream of army lorries and tracked vehicles came through Rhynie. I had never seen anything like it before and later discovered that it had something to do with D-Day. Ever since, my image of the build up to D-Day is of every road in Britain, even the remotest, absolutely crammed with the military, all pouring down south to get at the Germans.

That was almost the only formal link with soldiers and the hardware of war that I experienced as a child. Sometimes men in dark brown uniforms gathered in the village square and we children used to try to talk to them. They seemed nice and smiled at us, but they were foreign so we couldn't understand what they were saying. Someone told me they were Italian prisoners, presumably working on the farms round Rhynie. The real war as far as I was concerned took place in the pages of the *Beano*, which featured a cartoon character called 'Musso the Wop, He's a Big-a-da Flop' and his friend Adolf. Adolf was always surprised by the efforts of the Allies into exclaiming 'Himmel', translated by myself as a thoughtful 'Hmm'.

Origins

If in fantasy I were to release the rein on my desire, not an alternative easily open to someone burned with the brand of Calvin, I would spread my body over the hills of Strathbogie and lose all sense of self within that hard and beautiful soil. That is *my* home. My mother's origins were different, rooted in a small circle of farming country laid to the north of Bennachie and forming the parishes of Bourtie, Chapel of Garioch and Daviot.

In a hollow below Barra Hill stone circle lies Bourtie churchyard, with a selection of Lumsdens and Duncans interred there. I always imagine them, farmers and farm servants, as stolid children of the Picts who built the circle. This stolidity, lack of poetry, lack of imagination, is underlain by something more elusive which is caught in the writing of Lewis Grassic Gibbon and has to do with an inarticulate mystical feeling for the land. In Calvinist culture this can translate into intense desire for essence. Maggie Duncan Lumsden, who I think must have been at least a remote relative of mine, has these lines from Fiona MacLeod on her gravestone in Bourtie:

> I too will set my face to the wind
> And throw my handful of seed on high:
> It is loveliness I seek, not lovely things.

My grandfather, Innes Lumsden, had started out in life as a farm servant, probably in the Garioch, but came to Aberdeen where he worked in the saw mill of a timber yard. His marriage to my grandmother was a social advance because she was the daughter of a jobbing gardener. Unfortunately, one day at work he sawed the fingers off one of his hands and had to finish in that career. Family legend, which may be based on fact, records that he made his living in a variety of ways, working as a comic Irish singer in the Aberdeen Music Hall, as a waiter in the

Athenaeum on the Castlegate, as a caterer, and in 1913 he became the beadle of Queen's Cross church in the West End of Aberdeen, remaining there until 1948. When I knew him he was a dignified, bald, elderly man who, as part of his role in the church, regularly dressed in striped trousers and a black 'claw hemmer jecket', with the most fascinating item of all, a starched dickie on the front of his shirt which, when released, rolled up underneath his chin. When I was a small child he used to do this suddenly, making me start, and enquired, roaring with laughter, 'Did ah fleg ye, Davie lad?'

Grandad often wore a silk top hat, especially when he was officiating at funerals and on Sundays. I delighted in walking with him from the tenement where he lived in Holburn Street to the church, because he looked so grand and seemed to know so many people. As I trotted beside him he would entertain me with familiar jokes. 'Tak langer strides Dauvit, ye'r weerin'oot yer sheen ower quick', till we reached Queen's Cross.

In church on a Sunday I used to sit in the Gallery waiting for the most dramatic family occasion of the week. Shortly before the service started, my grandfather would appear in his full formal attire through a door near the centrally placed, dark, polished pulpit, carrying the Good Book. Then he would slowly march up the steps to lay the Book on the lectern with great care and correctness, descend erect and dignified, and disappear out of the door for a moment or two. Finally in this splendid liturgy, the minister would emerge and mount the pulpit, followed by granddad who would shut the gate and slide the 'sneck', locking the minister in place. It always felt to me that my grandfather was the real boss. This was confirmed for me by the fact that he disappeared through the door after the ritual, condescending to return only to listen to and in my eyes criticise the sermon, and finally to release the minister at the end of the service.

When I was ten, my parents decided I should continue my education in the city and we moved into a tenement in Union Grove in Aberdeen, round the corner from my grandparents on Holburn Street. I began attending the Sunday School at Queen's Cross church and spending much of my time at my grandparents' flat. Like the tenement in which I lived, the one inhabited by my grandparents was laid out in the manner typical of the city; at street level the main doorway with a bank of bell pulls on either side of the door; on each floor a pair of doors leading into flats, with a shared lavatory on each half-landing. The major gossiping stance was at the stair head. Conversation was often between families in adjacent flats, drawn together by the shared intimacy of a lavatory seat, the need to clean and provide paper for the lavatory, and the maintenance of the gas light on the landing.

My grandmother's kitchen always had the faint sour smell of escaping coal gas, which did not worry me particularly during the day. It obsessed me at night. Like most Aberdeen tenements, the kitchen cum living room had an alcove containing a bed, hidden behind a curtain. Sometimes I had to sleep there and felt sure that one day I would be found dead in the morning, overcome by gas. My grandmother set me regular tasks to keep me busy. For example, I would have to cut up old copies of newspapers for use in the lavatory, or I might have to fold sheets of the same paper into spills for lighting the gas lamps. The Aberdeen *Press and Journal* was quite suitable for use in the lavatory, followed by the *Evening Express* but *Bon Accord* was most unpleasant because of the shiny consistency of the paper. Grandma also frugally collected dry bread in a tin and every now and then I would be asked to grate it to make breadcrumbs. Across the dark corridor from the kitchen was the front room, or 'ben the hoose', which was very formal. It contained pot plants like Lily of the Valley and Aspidistra, and it had a piano. It was hardly ever used except for the celebration on New Year's Eve, though I used to spend a lot of time there, strumming on the piano and watching the trams droning and rattling by. The tram lines diverged just outside my first floor viewing stance. The drivers had to lean down from their position with a long lever to shift the rails with a clunk, one way or the other, to ensure that they either proceeded down Holburn Street to the Bridge of Dee or turned right up Great Western Road. I used to watch for hours, waiting for a driver to make a mistake, which occasionally he did.

My other childhood haunt in Aberdeen was at uncle Tom's. He was a shop assistant with the Co-op and he and my auntie Nan lived on the top floor of a big house on Carden Place opposite Queen's Cross Church. They occupied this privileged site because uncle Tom ran the Boys Circle Club and a Boys' Brigade Company, both sponsored by the church and occupying the premises lower down. Eventually he took over from granddad as beadle of the church. I was for a short time a member of the Circle Club, where manliness was the message. There was always a short service in the middle of the evening during which we sang tough hymns like 'Fight the good fight' and 'Onward Christian Soldiers, Marching as to War'. I remember repeated readings from *Corinthians I, Chapter 13* on faith, hope and charity, and St. Paul's reflection, 'When I was a child, I thought as a child... but now I am a man and have put away childish things'.

The world

Any fantasies I might have about forebears who were not horny handed sons and daughters of toil had to come from Hay side. They had a different, more worldly style than my mother's people. My great grandfather, Peter Hay, was a licensed victualler from Burntisland in Fife. He came north and opened a grocer's shop on the corner of Union Grove and Holburn Street. He had another son, half brother of my grandfather, who really did make it to the big time, ending up as Sir John Hay, the boss of Guthries the rubber people. Nobody on our side of the family knew him, because the brothers had fallen out very badly and would have nothing to do with each other. Eventually my cousin Peter, who did part of his National Service with a Highland regiment in Malaya in the late forties, sought out Sir John while he was there and was given a small financial advance.

My grandfather, also Peter Hay, was a seafaring man all his life and ensured that his three sons Peter, Oliver and John also went to sea. He had been the master of a square rigged sailing ship and had a reputation for bad temper. One day he stormed out of my grandmother's house and slammed the door so hard that the stained glass fell out and crashed on to the floor. He clearly disapproved of my mother, who claimed he never spoke a civil word to her, preferring to stare silently at the wall until she left. He died when I was very young and my memory of him is of a thin old man sitting up in bed in a dressing gown, speaking to me in the gentlest and kindest of tones. I suppose he must have been dying.

Grannie Hay was more earthbound, the daughter of a groom from Daviot. When she came to stay with us she made lumpy porridge. To me this symbolised a serious personality disorder, and I was foolish enough to tell her in my mother's presence, that I did not like her. The penalty for expressing what I am certain was also my mother's view, was to be locked in the lavatory to contemplate my sins. It was the first occasion on which I was aware of being a participant, albeit unwilling, in a Freudian defence mechanism.

My father worked for the Dundee, Perth and London Shipping Company. On one occasion after the war, I must have been about eleven, he took me with him on a trip on his ship, the *Clova* , which was a coaster trading up and down the North Sea between Dundee and London. Almost nothing of the trip remains with me, except the visit of an itinerant preacher aboard ship whilst we were docked in Dundee. My father had left me to my own devices and I was surprised by this man who urged on me the necessity to read the Bible. To ensure compliance he offered me a miniature Bible in return for a promise to read it every day for the rest of my life. I gave the necessary undertaking and preserved with my vow for a day or two.

When he returned and found out what had happened, my father gently warned me to keep clear of people like that. As a very young apprentice in the Merchant Service, he had been up to Archangel in North Russia at the time of the Revolution and had seen people starving in the streets. In his early thirties he visited Calcutta and came home with photographs of people so thin that I did not see anything like them again until the pictures began to come out of the Nazi concentration camps after the war. These experiences made him an extreme radical and suspicious of any religious or political establishment. He spoke with admiration of Lenin and foresaw the overthrow of capitalism, but politics to him was all to do with the heart. I assimilated my basic political emotions from him. Today, surveying the dreadful ruins of Eastern Europe, I find an equivocation in myself, because I remember his warmth and passion. It is not good when a Utopian vision is crushed and discredited. I wonder who will now speak for the defenceless poor.

Becoming Scottish

I do not entirely understand why Strathbogie wrenches so strongly at the heart, but perhaps it is to do with loss of innocence. Life in the city was much less lonely than in Rhynie, where I had been the clever but unpopular boy in the class. In Aberdeen I was amongst people who were my intellectual equals or better and I made friends that I still think of as friends today.

School in Aberdeen meant primarily the establishment of my identity as a Scotsman. I had of course been aware that the English were different. We in Rhynie knew that there were wealthy softies who came up from down south, with their politeness and their accents, to shoot grouse. They were careless with the expression of feeling. Once an Englishman and his young son had come to stay in the village. They caused general derision and some embarrassment when seen to kiss in public.

It was the notion of the English as a target for anger and envy that was new to me, and seemingly necessary for a clearly focused image of my nationality. In Aberdeen, at the emblematic level, nationhood tended to pivot round the Wallace Statue at the end of Union Terrace, where occasionally politicians would stand in front of a Saltire and harangue about independence. The maiden lady who was my first teacher at Aberdeen Grammar School seems to have had similar notions about Scotland's future. My memory of her is constituted by her presentation of a series of vignettes of history in which the iniquities of the English were made vividly clear to us.

To this day my knowledge of Scottish history is nothing more than a vague chauvinistic haze permeated by hostility to England and populated by Bruce, Wallace, Knox, The Covenanters, Mary Queen of Scots and Bonnie Prince Charlie (Oh yes, and Calvin, surely he was a Scot?) drifting in a confusion of dates and battlefields. What our teacher added as a bonus was the necessity for an element of revenge. Was it Wallace, or Bruce, or someone else? I don't remember; at any rate a patriot. One night he caught the English garrison unawares at Dunottar Castle and burned the lot of them alive. Thus we treat our enemies, boys. And if the need arises, will do so once again. 'Oh, flower of Scotland...'.

Well and truly cast out of Eden now, it is about this time I found out we weren't supposed to like Catholics and Jews either. Not that there were many in Aberdeen. But by chance, one of the boys in our year was a Catholic and irritated the teacher no end by having days off school to attend religious services. Another was Jewish and somehow I was given the impression that he wasn't really Scottish. Fury was welling up in the midst of us from some underground spring of passion and seeking its victims.

How strange that these were the targets through which anger found its substance. Five of my ten years had been lived through the nightmare struggle against Fascism which issued in the discovery of the Holocaust. I sat in the Majestic cinema on Union Street and saw the newsreels from Belsen when they first came out. This was a cry for vengeance if ever there was one, but I could not comprehend the hellish vision. My war was a small boy's fantasy fought in the pages of the *Beano*; anger in that direction was meaningless.

To my credit, I was bewildered by my teacher's anger with Jews and Catholics. But I was definitely unsure about the English. In 1948 my father finally left the sea, his health broken by his wartime experiences, and bought a smallholding in Devon. And so it came about that the boarding house door closed behind me at Queen Elizabeth's School. I was alone in the shiny corridor with my trunk and the polite English lady and, for the first time, I felt a tight-lipped rage boiling up in me against my father.

The Landscape in the Mind

Stuart Hood

Wordsworth believed that to grow up in the country is in some way ennobling and purifying. Nature, as he puts it in one of the *Lyrical Ballads* of 1798, 'has a world of ready wealth/our minds and souls to bless.' On that score I should perhaps count myself lucky to have spent my first eleven years in Edzell in the county of Angus and to have been free to play in the surrounding fields and woods and by the river that runs past the village.

I cannot believe, however, that my experience of the countryside bore any relationship to that of the ploughmen's children with whom I went to school. They came from bare cottar houses set usually in bleak gardens where the stalks of sprouts, kale and cabbages, were often the only vegetation. They had to walk two, three or even four miles to school where in winter they arrived soaked. One of my enduring memories is of the smell of clothes drying in front of the fire in the classroom where my father taught. They came from families whom at term time I had seen flitting, perched in a cart that was piled with their few bits of furniture and sheltering from the November rain under a tarpaulin. When I went for walks with my parents they would watch us from their doors and vanish inside or round the back of the house to avoid having to greet my father, the dominie, whose strict discipline they endured in school. In the autumn during the 'potato holidays' they were used as cheap labour by the local farmers. As I cycled past I saw them make their way along the drills bent over to collect the crop the mechanical digger threw up. Theirs was, I was aware, a different existence from mine. Nature to them meant something different.

When we were together in the school playground, what they could communicate were certain country skills such as how to guddle trout in the little burns, how to make a *peerie* – a top – from an old cotton reel, how to make a whistle from a sucker from a tree, how to find pignuts.

But they were also familiar with the harsher side of country life – how lambs were '*libbed*', how a hen's neck was thrawn, how a rabbit was killed. They were liable to harry nests in the hedgerows. They were, in short, totally unsentimental about nature and its creatures. Nature was there, they lived in it and accepted it. They would leave school to work in it at the tail of the plough. To me, on the other hand, the countryside was a continual source of interest, of discovery and pleasure. It spelt freedom and adventure. I escaped into it from the oppressive care of my mother and a cossetted existence.

From an early age I was aware of water. There was the North Esk – or the North Water as some people still called it, which was etymologically correct since 'esk' is the Gaelic *uisge* for 'water'. Above the village where the river was caught between the cliffs of the Highland Fault there were the salmon loups where the gleaming fish hurled themselves upstream against the rush of the water, fell back into the foam and rose again, driven by some physiological need to reach the breeding grounds far up the glen. Further down it settled into deep brown and amber pools, still and lazy, flecked with foam. Where it widened out, grew shallower to skirt the village, a dam diverted some of the flow into a lade that drew off water to drive the wheels of a tweed mill and a flour mill. Once as a small child I was taken to the tweed mill and shown how the great wheel drove the noisy looms. The banks of the lade leaked here and there and were rich with myrrh and globe flowers. To cross to the other side of the river you had to take a foot bridge – the shakin brig – suspended over the river by steel cables on which we climbed and swung. From it you could fish for trout and watch the salmon nosing up river, leaping to shake off the sea-lice, or drifting downstream, spent, sometimes trailing a deadly yellow fungus. When there was a spate the water rose brown and loud bearing down branches and once a dead roe deer. In hard winters there was a skin of ice over the still pools.

In summer when 'the visitors', who usurped our favourite spots and whom we village children despised for having nannies, came from Edinburgh or Dundee to spend their holidays we would wait till they were halfway over the river and then swing on the cables till the whole bridge swayed. Then 'the visitors' clung to the sides in fear. So we had our revenge on the outsiders and punished them for their otherness.

Below the bridge was the ford where the horses and carts came over in summer to avoid the way round the Lang Stracht, the long straight road that lay across the river in Kincardineshire and led to the Gannochy Bridge a mile above the village. The big Clydesdales plunged in with their feathered hooves until the water came up to their bellies and the axles of the carts. They clattered out, shaking off the water, and climbed up the 'Gassy Brae' past the gasworks and on to the smiddie. Sometimes they were brought in there to be shod and you could watch the aproned smith at work. If he was in a good temper he might allow you to work the long handle of the bellows till the metal was brought to a white heat. Then he drew it from the fire and shaped it into a shoe to the clangour of his anvil and among a shower of sparks. When he tempered the shoe by plunging it into a pail of cold water the water bubbled and steamed. Then came the moment when the patient beast allowed him to lift a foot, catch it between his knees and fit the hot shoe before he drove in the long nails to secure it. The smell of burning hoof was unforgettable.

On the bend of the river were sandstone cliffs on which we climbed and from which I one day fell some forty feet landing, fortunately, feet first in a deep pool from which I emerged with a couple of bruises. It is a moment which returns to me still from time to time with a *frisson* of fear.

Besides the North Esk there was the West Water which came down from Glen Lethnot, spilled over a fall and was channelled between sand stone rocks into deep pools where I caught my first trout. There was the pleasurable fear of crossing it by a narrow plank bridge over a deep pool – the Pirners's Brig built by members of the firm of Coates of Paisley, whose name I knew from the pirns, the cotton reels, in my mother's work-basket. Sometimes tinkers were encamped there in benders or caravans. Once a tinker's horse got on to the bridge, slipped and straddled the planks. It had to be pushed over into the river from which it splashed out unharmed. Perhaps my favourite stream, however, was the Mooran Burn that gathered the water from the hillsides of the Wirren and Bulg, ran down between steep sides and under a stone bridge to join the Esk.

Here – as by the West Water – there was a picnic place to which the women and children went in an open carriage and the men on bicycles. On the grass above the water a fire was built to brew tea. While the men went off to explore or fish the women spread out the contents of the picnic baskets – home made scones, sponges, cakes, sandwiches, bottles of lemonade – on rugs and clothes. After a while the men would be summoned back to eat. The meal over, there were games of cricket and rounders in which men, women and children joined. There were rituals such as that on the way to the Mooran – not far past a clump of standing stones – where we stopped so that I could drink from a spring by the roadside. Sheep with curled horns watched as I stooped over the splashing water to drink and fled when I rose and waved my arms. Why, we often wondered, should the Mooran picnics have been so often interrupted by rain that made us run for cover while the thunder rattled among the hills. When we got home, were changed and dried, there would be a kitchen sink full of brown trout, beautiful, smooth, speckled.

Nearer home – not far from the bottom of our garden in fact – there was the Wishop Burn. (The Lindsays – whose red sandstone castle with its Renaissance pleasance lay beyond the village out on the road to the kirkyard (the way the hearse took with the men walking behind in their tophats) – had had the feudal power of pit and gallows and their own executioner to whom they had granted fishing rights in the stream.) Tamed now and fishless it ran on through the woods outside the village which concealed a mound – the Gallows Knap – where no doubt the executioner had done his work. Its banks were riddled with the holes of water 'rats' (actually harmless voles) which we pursued with sticks and stones – ineffectually I am glad to say – simply because they were rats. Water was connected in my mind with pleasure, with play and adventure.

Our territory was limited to the immediate surroundings of the village but could be extended by occasional expeditions by bicycle – over the river to the abandoned airfield by the Lang Stracht among woods rich in blaeberries (here in the First World War there had been American airmen and – but was this possible? – Chinese labourers); or over the West Water to the White Caterthun, the Iron Age hilltop fort from which we could look down on the strath and up into the Howe of the Mearns. To the north was the Mounth which had historically been the mountain barrier between Lowlands and Highlands. To the south the strath stretched down towards Montrose, Arbroath, Dundee and the Firth of Tay, beyond which you could see how the East Neuk of Fife nosed darkly into the North Sea. On a clear day the Bell Rock lighthouse was a white gleam where sea and sky met. I could imagine the Roman galleys sailing up off-shore in support of the legions that had camped just beyond Stracathro before they marched on to the battle of Mons Graupius somewhere in or beyond the hills of the Mounth. I was looking, although I did not know it till later, into Pictish country where the men in strange pointed hats on their ponies had left stones rich in symbols and carvings. This was a landscape in which I felt and still feel at home. I have asked for my ashes to be scattered within the stone ramparts of the fort from which as a child I looked down with a kind of wonder.

In that landscape I learned to be observant: to be aware of a sudden movement like the flash of a wing that betrayed a bird when it broke from cover; to know that a rabbit or hare would squat unmoving, unseen, until you almost trod on it; that a grouse or a pheasant would wait to the last moment before rising with a clatter of wings from under your feet. These were habits of observation which I had recourse to in very different landscapes. Trekking down from the Lombardy plain through the high Apennines, far behind the German lines in the autumn and winter of 1943, I could tell the lie of the land from the way the water ran, knew when I had reached a watershed, could guess how the paths would run. At moments of danger I knew that if I sat very still in cover I might not be noticed and that what I had to avoid was a sudden tell tale movement. Later in my odyssey, walking through the woods of Tuscany long after curfew on some Partisan errand – the Germans were everywhere and the dark was safer than the day – I might be startled when I almost trod on a pheasant but its rowdy flight was familiar, reassuring. Through this time I carried with me in my mind a compass in which the north was marked by the line of the High Street in Edzell. It pointed to the hills above which on various times, coming back at night, I had seen the merry dancers, the Northern Lights, the *aurora borealis*, like iridescent veils fluttering in the night sky. The map of the village was like a template which I laid on other landscapes in Africa and Italy to orient myself, find the north star and set my course.

At the bottom of our street was the station where the little steam engines in the blue livery of the Caledonian Railway brought in the occasional two- or three-carriage passenger trains or shunted waggons to and fro. Very occasionally a train driver would let me come on board as he manoeuvred in the shunting yard. There was a smell of oil, of coal and steam and a blast of heat from the stokehole. In 1926 there was a week without trains but to me as a child the General Strike was remote, unfathomable, uninteresting.

If I took with me from my Angus childhood a certain closeness to nature I also learned to accept in a matter of fact way that animals were killed and eaten, like the cow with the butcher walking slowly behind it as it made its way up the high street to the slaughter house just beyond the village, like the grouse laid by the brace, hundreds at a time, when the ponies came down off the moors in the shooting season, like the occasional hare or pheasant that the gamekeeper laid at our door in recognition of my father's social standing. Watching my mother skin and gut rabbits or pluck and draw a chicken I learned not be squeamish.

From an early age I knew that it is possible to understand and speak more than one language to say the same thing in two totally different ways and to understand both. At home, my parents insisted on standard English albeit with a Scots accent. But in the playground and in the village street I heard and spoke Scots and specifically that variant of it which substitutes *f* for *wh*. So it was natural to say *faur* for *where* and *fou* for *who* and to have at my command a lexicon to which I can refer in my mind but which I can no longer use – for who of those with whom I now communicate would know the meaning of *forfauchen*, *wee boukit*, *shilpit*, *wabbit oot;* of *sharn* and *feich*, what it means to *teem* a barrel or to *ca* a rope. Sometimes and in some contexts it was permissible at home or in company to use words from this lexicon but only so to speak in inverted commas to indicate that the speaker knew that they were not received usage. This bilingualism, I believe, is what led to my interest in languages, in their similarities and differences, their idiosyncrasies and various riches. I learned too that some words are untranslatable. There was the word *drouth*. 'There's no drouth today,' my mother would say as she gathered in the still damp washing from the backgreen. What was the English equivalent certainly not 'drought'. And how to translate *drouthie* as in 'he's drouthie' where the word speaks metaphorically of the desert within a man that must be watered with alcohol.

Entertainment for children in the village was usually self generated. It meant learning to strip and oil a bicycle, to tend a carbide bicycle lamp, to tie a cast of trout flies, to shape bows and arrows, assemble kites, build bracken 'forts' in the woods to be defended with a hail of pine cones, to play *bools* in the street or against a wall. The most treasured *bools* were large, made of glass and filled somehow with coloured filaments; together with the smaller plain coloured ones – brown, blue or red – they were carried in a little bag my mother had made for me. Because it would have been not proper for the dominie's child to ask for pennies I was not allowed to join the masked guisers on Hallowe'en; a restriction I resented. In a different way I resented having to go to dancing-classes in the village hall where the teacher as he put us through our steps played on a little fiddle which was, I suppose, what is called a kit. At the dancing classes there were not many of us – and then mostly girls; my school friends were noticeably absent. My mother sat watching with other mothers in the village hall and added to my embarrassment. Above them hung a large monochrome picture – an improbably (indeed impossible) rendering of the charge of the Scots Greys at Waterloo.

Most summers' entertainment arrived from outside. Once it was a troop of horse artillery which encamped on the Muir – the common at the top of the village – with bugle calls and horses that leapt hurdles of broom. More usually it was a circus, with piebald ponies and an elephant that left great round turds. There was sometimes a fair as well, with shooting booths where the targets were small balls that danced on a jet of water and my brother once won a coconut. But the real fair, which I was not allowed to attend because it would have meant being absent from school, was at Trinity halfway to Brechin. I envied those of the boys who brazenly absented themselves and came back with little badges they had won stuck in their jackets.

It was on the Muir that I first saw moving pictures. I was sitting on a cushion on the grass in a tent attached to the end of a caravan which had a port in it through which film was projected. The proprietor was Mr Bingo, who lived in the caravan alongside his projector and his cans of film. Where he had got the bits and pieces – he showed bits of Westerns, bits of Chaplin – I cannot imagine; but they fascinated me. When he and his horse had moved we would scour the grass and hope to find a frame or two he had discarded. We had no idea that it was 35mm nitrate film and therefore inflammable. Fortunately my mother did not know either or

I would have not been so early captivated by a medium which still fascinates me.

The cultural centre of the village was the village hall, vaguely Scottish baronial in concept, with a tower and a clock with a Westminster chime. It had been built by a local man who had become a leading figure in the Stock Exchange. Along with the building he had presented a complete library where I would look through bound volumes of some illustrated paper the *Illustrated London News*, I suppose – full of black and white illustrations of events, battles, politicians, marvels which I loved without having any real understanding of them or any context into which I might fit them.

In the hall my father organised lantern lectures – of which I remember one on the archaeology of Dunottar Castle and another on the stars. Here too I saw my first play: *Campbell of Kilmore*. It was set in the aftermath of the '45 and the repression inspired by the Duke of Cumberland. On a visit to my mother's birthplace near Nairn I had been to Culloden and seen the graves of clans and the Well of the Dead. I knew the sentimental songs the Edinburgh ladies wrote about Bonnie Prince Charlie and was a sentimental Jacobite. I leapt in my seat when a fugitive Jacobite who refuses to break under interrogation is taken out and a shot is heard. It was my first experience of the power of the make-believe of the stage.

The players were actors from the Arts League of Service – itinerants who arrived with a van for their properties and costumes to present mime and song as well as one act plays. I remember a mime, based on what I now believe to have been a piece by Lope de Vega, in which Death and Cupid accidentally exchange their arrows with tragic and comical effects. They mimed too to old songs like 'The Laird of Cockpen' or 'Get up and bar the door'. From their singer, who wore a kind of monk's habit, I heard – without knowing it – my first lieder.

The hall was also the centre of more social occasions – soirées (sworries we called them) – at which you got a bag at the door containing a scone or a cake and sweets, and tea was served from big urns. There were games and dancing for the grown-ups. At Christmas time there was a pine tree supplied, I imagine, by one of the estates round about. It reached up almost to the roof of the big hall bearing a present for every child in the village. I have no idea – it was not a question that interested me – who funded the occasion and bought the presents. Childhood is an age of unknowing, of mysteries that are accepted and not questioned – a time when our vision of life is a kind of tunnel vision.

In my case this sense of life as mystery was no doubt accentuated by illnesses of an unspecified kind which I was assured brought me 'to death's door.' But in that age before antibiotics illness was a more serious matter than it is today. What was perceived as my 'delicate' condition meant that I spent a great deal of time alone in bed, or convalescing, reading, fashioning lanterns and boxes and toys from wallpaper taken from old pattern books, building models with Meccano, playing complicated games of patience. I was a centre of interest and attention. It was a condition which I both savoured and fretted against. The point came, fortunately, when I decided that I was going to escape from what Robert Louis Stevenson calls 'the land of counterpane.'

That decision, that change, was contemporaneous with our move to Montrose. I was now twelve. Although it was only some fifteen miles from Edzell, I had been in the town only once. In those days travel was difficult and not lightly undertaken by bus or train; my parents were in any case thrifty. I was four or five at the time of that visit and remember chiefly being frightened by a seal which had been caught in the salmon nets and kept as a pet in a fish factory. It came splashing out of a tank and made me take refuge behind my mother.

It was difficult to adapt to the town after village life. There was a perceived loss of freedom for there were no longer woods and fields within easy reach. Now I had to come to terms with a different landscape and, above all, to become aware of the sea. At night in winter as I lay in bed I could hear the waves drumming on the beach. It was from over the sea that the skeins of wild geese came in over the town, strung out against the sky, calling stridently as they flew to land in the mudflats of the Basin.

Occasionally I managed to get permission from the owner of a lug sailed boat to sail with him up into the Basin or down the estuary towards where the tide and the river met and rose up in waves at the harbour bar. I saw the fishermen's wives, speaking their own dialect, sitting in their doors in Ferryden across the river from the town, baiting the long lines which they coiled in creels. Sometimes I would go down to the quayside and buy fish fresh from the sea when the boats came in. These were inshore boats with a little wheelhouse; further out you could see the trawlers and drifters with their smoke stacks and brown sails tossing against the horizon. Along the beach the salmon nets were strung out on poles that ran two or three hundred yards into the water. The salmon came nosing along the net and found themselves in a great arrowheaded trap. The fishermen clambered out on the ropes and scooped them out. On the platform in the railway station the fish boxes waited to be loaded on the train south – to the cities where they ate salmon and crabs and lobsters. Sometimes fish trains would come through – from Aberdeen presumably – smelling strongly, and leaking water from the melting ice packed round the fish. Here the engines had a different livery – the green of the London and North Eastern Railway. We got to know the silhouettes of the locomotives with their aerodynamic lines and snorting power. These were the machines that would one day take me to Edinburgh, to London, to freedom.

The landscape I came to know and appreciate was that of the links and sand dunes which ran far along to the mouth of the North Esk under the cliffs of St Cyrus. Below the cliffs there was a fisherman's hut with a freshwater spring in the dunes where their black cobles were drawn up. On summer days a moment could come when the sun was suddenly obscured, the temperature dropped and a haar came slowly in from the sea, thick and white.

It was a landscape on which there lay a light that had a special and extraordinary quality. In it a cartwheel threw a precise shadow on the ground that seemed to engage with the wheel that made it. In the late summer it lasted long into the north west and shone in layers of peacock colour over the waters of the Basin and the hills beyond. In late September it gave a particular glow to the light yellow and brown of the sand of the long beach and the dunes where, along with other fortunate friends, I waited for the day to come when I should leave, go south to Edinburgh and University.

In Edzell I had been used to snow, to waking to a padded silence and knowing that overnight the snow had fallen inches deep, to go walking in it along roads where the wind had piled the drifts high up against the telephone poles, to see the tracks of birds and animals on the surface. There seemed to be less snow in Montrose although it could be cold; but there were frosts and the curling pond on the Links froze over. Then a boy and girl from the top class at the Academy would go to the Rector and ask for a skating holiday, which was usually granted. But the most exciting skating was on Duns Dish on Huntly Hill where there were fires on the bank, the curling stones thundered on the ice and I skated hand in hand in a state of innocent exhilaration with a girl from my class.

Montrose was the locus of my adolescence with its fears and uncertainties, its ignorance and vague intimations of adulthood. The town society was not one that one could easily enter and my family were not socially skilled. As a result I felt an outsider who had some contact with young people of my own age because of school or because we played golf together; but I was not part of that network of relationships and friendships into which they had been born.

I grew up in a society whose members did not communicate readily. In German they say that a person is *wortkarg* – stingy with words. I remember the laconic exchanges of the Angus ploughmen, that 'Aye, man,' which was their ritual greeting, their terse mode of recognition of another human being's existence. What the social and historical factors were that fashioned this reticence or the sardonic humour to which it sometimes extended I do not know. What I have learned is that, in the West, people have other kinds of discourse which I first came across in the Glasgow tram driver who slept next to me in the barrackroom and who, when we were issued with a bayonet, wept and apostrophised this fucking thing with which we were supposed to kill human beings. Perhaps the east coast territory of my boyhood lay on the wrong side of the Highland line, so that we were untouched by the tradition of story telling and verbalisation which the Highlanders and the Irish brought with them to the industrial towns of the West. Perhaps that is why I have, from time to time in my life, been accused of being uncommunicative, reticent. Perhaps I merely bear the stamp of my upbringing, my childhood and the East coast youth.

From that youth one of my constant memories is of a huge overarching expanse of sky spanning the landscape from the line of the horizon out at sea to the hills of the north and west. It is a landscape in which I am alone.

YE CANNA BIDE IN A KIRK!

Cathie Imlah

My early years were spent in what to me as a child were almost perfect surroundings. I lived with my parents and elder brother Alex in a small cottage which was one of several at Hillhead, West Cults. The cottages have long since been demolished and the area rebuilt.

I loved the woods at the back of our house where Edie and Betty my two little friends, and I spent hours roaming amongst the bracken quite hidden from view. There were quite a number of hollows amongst the bracken which added to the novelty. We would then reappear dusty but happy and head for home our stomachs telling us it was meal time.

There was another wooded area of conifers near by known as the 'private wood', where the trees grew so thickly that very little light filtered through. We seldom ventured in there as it was so dark and ominous. To add to our apprehension we discovered a hut constructed of branches and intertwined greenery. We didn't linger to find out if it had an occupant or not. During our wanderings through the woods and along the roadsides we sampled many plants and berries, yet I can never recall any ill effects. The tiny peas of the tufted vetch known as 'birdies peas' were enjoyed, and 'soorocks' or sorrel was chewed with relish. We climbed gean trees for wild cherries, often breaking branches in our efforts to reach them. Blaeberries were more difficult to find as the 'cushies' (wood pigeons) often got there first, their purple-stained droppings telling the tale.

At the edge of the wood there was a grassy clearing with a stretch of water known as the 'pondie'. In the spring we would set forth with glass jars suspended from string handles. Into the jars we would scoop the jelly substance containing frogs' spawn and bear them homewards, where they had little hope of ever maturing into frogs, the jar very often being knocked over or forgotten about; another fate of the poor tadpole was to be gobbled up by its siblings! I found looking for birds' nests a fascinating pastime and delighted in finding a thrush's nest with its blue speckled eggs, or a tiny wren's nest in an upturned tree root.

Another occasional treat for us girls was provided by one of Edie's elder brothers. He was employed as a shop message boy in Cults and was permitted to use the shop cycle to and from work. The cycle was specially designed with a small wheel in front, above which was a small metal frame to hold a large basket. Into this basket was stowed all the provisions for delivery to the shop's customers.

However, sometimes it had a rather different role when Edie's brother took us for a jaunt in the basket. There was only room for one at a time, but we thoroughly enjoyed wobbling along a path at the edge of a field, through a moor of whins and broom near Earls Wells and Dathebity House. We then wended our way through a number of beech trees the wheels scrunching the beech mast. Tree roots made the trip more hazardous and sometimes resulted in spills but never any serious injuries. When we were dusted down we clambered into the basket to bump our way back to join the others.

At the bottom of the field in front of our house was what to us was a large cairn of stones (it is now surrounded by houses in Bieldside). We scrambled about quite a lot amongst the stones imagining piles of bodies hidden underneath after some bloody affray. Who knows we may have been right, as the cairn is now listed as an ancient monument.

My father had a beautiful garden abundant with hollyhocks, carnations, pansies, Sweet Williams and roses to name but a few. He also grew a whole range of fruit and vegetables as well. I particularly remember parsnips, as I didn't like them, but I was advised by my mother to eat them 'as they were good for me'. I had my own little garden where I sowed a packet of mixed flower seeds intended for a child's garden. Sometimes, if I thought the seedlings were taking too long to appear, I would go investigating with my little trowel – usually with disastrous results, much to my father's annoyance.

When confined indoors for various reasons I enjoyed reading, drawing and colouring with crayons. I also liked wielding a scissors, cutting out pictures from a selection of catalogues, magazines and comics which I would stick into scrapbooks. At other times I would stick the cut outs on cardboard which would enable a figure to stand up. These could be used later in some imaginary game.

I attended Cults Primary School for three years where the school roll had a varied selection of scholars. These ranged from the sons and daughters of former tea planters and wealthy businessmen who went on later to fee paying schools, to cottage and cottar bairns. We as children seemed to integrate very well, but some teachers were inclined to favour the upper classes.

However, unknown to me this blissful existence was about to end. For a number of years my father had been part-time beadle at Cults West Church as well as being a gardener. In the summer of 1936 my father applied for the post of full time church officer at John Knox's Church, Mounthooly in Aberdeen and was chosen as the person most suitable. After discussing it with my mother, as she was to be involved in the catering side of the various church organisations, they decided to accept the post.

Although my parents were both country born and lovers of the rural scene, as I grew older I could understand why they moved to their new urban environment. Our country cottage had no indoor water supply. This had to be carried in pails from a communal water tap near the back of our house and, of course, after varied household uses it had to be carried out again. The toilet was a 'dry lavvie' in the garden and there was no electricity.

Their new accommodation had hot and cold running water, a WC, central heating, electric power and light. Also a Triplex fireplace in tiles and chrome, a great contrast to the old black fireplace which had to be burnished with Zebo black lead polish and emery paper. A small gas ring sat on the fire place ready to quickly boil up a kettle or pan.

I quite enjoyed a jaunt into town with my parents for new clothes, or better still if it meant a visit to the Rubber Shop on Netherkirkgate where I could spend my pocket money in the Toy Department. There on display behind plate glass sliding doors was a large selection of metal farm and wild animals painted in lifelike colours. I loved to play imaginary games with these animals and I was always keen to add to my collection. Our mission completed we would then board the blue Alexander's bus and head for home. Although we lived quite a distance from the bus route, I didn't mind the walk back home.

I was quite used to being inside a church because of my father's duties as a beadle at Cults West Church, but actually living in one was a different matter!

I really cannot recall much about our 'moving' day, probably because I was in shock, the contrast was so great between our two homes. A large door at street level was our entrance. One flight of grey stone stairs went upwards to the church, vestry and session room, then proceeded further up to the church gallery which also housed the huge church organ and choir. The downstairs flight led to the church hall and our flat which was actually in the 'sunks' – the Basement. The flat consisted of three rooms off a passage which led to the boiler house. The windows were quite large but as only about a quarter of the window came above the metal brander covering the sunks it wasn't much advantage. One thing I was not very keen on was the view from the windows, as we were only a few feet from the gravestones in the little churchyard attached to John Knox's Church. However, I soon got used to that but I was a bit apprehensive if a grave was opened next to our windows and I could see a pile of soil and wooden planks covering the grave ready for the burial next day!

When I first attended Causewayend School, which was quite near Mounthooly, the class roll was fifty two pupils and they were very different from my class mates at Cults. However, they were quite friendly and on learning my address they chorused, 'Bit ye canna bide in a kirk!' in tones of mixed disbelief, horror and amazement. Later on was my turn to be amazed when one classmate told the teacher that milk came from the 'Co-opie Dairy'. She was blissfully ignorant of how it originated.

About a month after we moved into town, I became seriously ill with nephritis, a disease of the kidneys. I was whisked away to the Sick Children's Hospital where I spent six weeks. At that time hospital visits were strictly supervised and a visitor's card had to be shown at the hospital entrance. It would have been easier to get into Fort Knox than pass the stern uniformed man in charge! However, I was so ill at first that my parents were allowed to visit at any time, and I really don't remember much about it. Later on during my stay I can recall being wakened at 5.30 a.m. to have my hands and face washed, followed by breakfast of scrambled eggs and toast. I can also remember the day I had my tonsillectomy. I was wheeled along the corridor to the operating theatre on a trolley. On the way we passed another patient returning to the ward after surgery. I could hear horrid gurgling noises which did nothing for my nerves as I was already very scared, although I would never have told anyone. In the theatre I was gently lifted on to the operating table where I could see what looked like a whirling light above my head. A white-coated figure asked me to open my mouth and placed something between my teeth; this was followed by a mask over my face, then oblivion. I regained consciousness a few hours later suffering from a very sore throat. I was so glad to be awake again it didn't really bother me all that much. I was discharged two weeks later with various 'do's' and 'don'ts' including 'no swimming' which to me was a great disappointment. When I grew up I realised how lucky I was to recover completely from such a serious illness. Two of my little fellow patients were not so fortunate as they died before reaching adulthood.

About two years later I had a second spell in hospital when I caught scarlet fever. This time my departure by ambulance was to the City Hospital in Urquhart Road, which was the town's hospital for all infectious diseases. At that time there was quite an epidemic and beds were in short supply, resulting in my being admitted to a side ward off the male scarlet fever ward. This I shared with a female nurse who had contracted rheumatic fever after scarlet fever and a four year old boy named John Cunningham who was an expert at both shuffling and playing cards.

I quite enjoyed my stay in hospital apart from the huge needle which was stuck in my bottom a short while after my admittance, and occasional doses of *cascara sagrada*, a vile-tasting laxative. Even acid drops handed round by the nurse didn't mask the taste of the revolting stuff. Every day we had a visit from the hospital matron, a small stoutish figure dressed in navy blue with a flowing white cap. She was accompanied by a retinue of white coated followers which included doctors and the ward sister. She spoke to every patient and enquired after their welfare, then placed a couple of sugar lumps on everyone's locker. I never discovered the reason for the sugar lumps – perhaps it was to boost our energy. It certainly had that effect on sister's day off as far as the young male patients in our main ward were concerned. Those patients who were on the mend got out of bed and chased the young probationer nurses round the ward. I remember particularly a young man with black curly hair who used to serenade one young nurse with the following popular song at that time:

> You can't stop me from kissin' you
> You can't stop me from cuddlin' too
> You can say no, no, no, that's all right
> I'll get even with you tonight
> 'Cause you can't stop me from dreamin'.

This was accompanied by much rolling of his eyes and great merriment from the rest of the ward, not to mention the young nurse's embarrassment! At visiting times only the minister was allowed to enter the wards after having donned a white coat. All other visitors had to stand outside the ward windows and try to carry on a mimed and gesticulating conversation which was rather frustrating for both patient and visitor!

When I got used to it, I spent quite a lot of my time in the small churchyard next to the church. I studied all the inscriptions and should anyone come looking for a certain grave, I was able to lead them to it. I became very friendly with Mr Middleton the gravedigger, who came when the grass needed cutting and to tidy up the graves. His services were also required when a grave had to be dug, but I gave the churchyard a wide berth when that was taking place. Mr Middleton was the first person I had ever seen with a glass eye. He quite often gave me a graphic description of how he lost it whilst splitting wooden canes with an axe.

During the winter my parents were kept very busy with the various church organisations. The youth organisations were the Marigolds (the junior branch of the Girls' Guildry), who wore yellow dresses, white berets and socks; the Girls' Guildry; the Lifeboys (the junior branch of the Boys' Brigade); and of course the Boys' Brigade. There was a Bowling Club and a Badminton Club also meetings of the Women's Leisure Hour and Women's Guild. The latter two meetings had tea served to their members which was a task left to my mother. In the hall kitchen two large copper urns were filled and brought to the boil then several packets of tea were emptied into the butter muslin bags which were tied with a draw string and placed in the bubbling water. Innumerable cups, saucers and plates had to be taken from the cupboards and set out on trays. The ladies then distributed a variety of sandwiches, cakes and biscuits to be consumed by their fellow members, washed down with cups of tea. After all this the dirty crockery had to be washed and stored away.

Above our flat was the minister's vestry and the session room. Around the walls of the vestry were hung the portraits of former ministers of the church – not a smile amongst them. One very happy assistant minister we had for a time was Alex Robertson, a Glaswegian, who entered the ministry later in life. He had a tremendous rapport with the youth of the church and was an officer in the Boys' Brigade. He had a fine baritone voice and was very fond of singing 'I'll Walk Beside You'. He always called me Catriona and used to say he would like to perform the wedding service when I got married. Sad to say he had gone south and I had lost touch with him by that time.

During the day the session room was the office of the church secretary, Mrs Mary Watson, who became a very dear friend of both my mother and I. She was a little, plump, very pleasant person, always immaculately dressed in variations of navy and white. She was widowed quite young and had a daughter Margaret a couple of years older than me.

My father was a man of many talents although I didn't appreciate it as a child. When the church drama club required a back cloth he would paint an appropriate scene. If paper flowers were required for the Junior Choir operettas he would make those as well. Most of all he loved wood, his hands running over its surface as he worked with it was like a caress. The son of a carpenter he never served on an apprenticeship, but he produced an array of beautiful wooden pieces in his life time.

When we moved into town my father spent quite a while searching for a suitable place in the church buildings which he could use as a workshop in his spare time. He finally settled for a large cupboard under a stairway – it didn't compare with his roomy workshop at Cults but it would suffice. He also read very widely and would often have deep discussions and arguments with the minister.

My mother and I spent many happy evening hours playing the gramophone listening to recordings of Bud and Joe Billings (on the Regal Zonophone label) and Arthur Tracy 'The Street Singer', one of my mother's favourites. I liked to play Harry Gordon's 'Beadle o' the Kirk' which I thought was most appropriate. If the gramophone spring did eventually snap after many hours of playing, it was taken to a music shop where it was fitted with a new spring at a very reasonable cost and carried off home again.

A favourite evening drink in our household was Rowntrees cocoa. For quite a while there was a free gift known as a CoCo Cub in every tin. These were small lead animals, painted in brightly coloured clothing, with such names as Silas Sly the fox and Henrietta Henspeckle, complete with poke bonnet.

Cigarette cards were another collectable item; these covered a wide spectrum – wild flowers, garden flowers, birds, fish and film stars, to name but a few. I gleaned quite a lot of information from these cards over a period of time.

One of my greatest joys was when I discovered the City's Children's Library. I spent many happy hours browsing through the bookshelves. Quite a number of the books were leather bound and it was a joy to handle them before exploring their contents: The atmosphere was entirely different to the bright cheery present day library. We always spoke in whispers and were afraid to cough or sneeze. If someone dropped a book it was almost a cardinal sin!

Across the street from the church were tenements which housed nine or ten families each. There was a wide variety of shops including John Junor newsagent, Mrs Mackay's Post Office and chemist, Forbes Wright hairdresser and A and A Douglas, butcher. The Co-op had a grocer, butcher and bakery store on the Gallowgate, while across the street was Brown the grocer. Around the corner on Causewayend was a small police station, Michie the grocer and Carcone's chip shop where youngsters could get a generous helping of chips for a halfpenny. Then as a final touch there was Ben Cormack the undertaker, so our needs were well supplied without venturing down town.

By 1939 the war clouds were gathering which was to alter our whole way of life. My brother Alex, who was a number of years older than me, was one of the first to enlist in the army. I can still see him holding up his racing cycle and remarking 'I won't be needing this for a while.' His prophecy certainly proved to be true, as he would see action at Dunkirk, North Africa, Italy and Greece before he came home thankfully unscathed in 1945. When war was declared everyone was issued with ration books, identity cards and gas masks. At school we had to wear our gas masks for short periods during lessons. Unfortunately for me, my gas-mask was the only one that made a 'raspberry' noise as I breathed out – this caused sniggering in the classroom, which inevitably got me into trouble.

Air raid shelters built of brick or concrete began to sprout up all over the city, which included school playgrounds. If an air raid warning went during school hours, we all trooped out to the shelters to sit on wooden benches until the 'all clear' sounded. Any scholar seen going into the shelter at any other time was usually given the belt. They were certainly very popular with the local tom cats, but there was little anyone could do about that.

I enjoyed secondary school most of the time, although mathematics was not my favourite subject. One of my maths teachers would hook his fingers into his waistcoat, peer over his horn rimmed glasses, then ask me 'Do you understand that Catherine?' If my answer was in the affirmative, he would announce to the class 'We can now assume the whole class understands!'

If an air raid alert went off between the hours of 10.00 p.m. and 6.00 a.m. school didn't commence until 10.00 a.m. next day, which was greeted with great glee by most of the scholars.

It was said that Aberdeen qualified as the most bombed city in Scotland. However, as the raids were often carried out by one or two aeroplanes in a hit and run sortie (very often without an air raid warning) the damage was small compared to the city of Glasgow.

The bombing raids began in the summer of 1940. I can well recall going out after lunch and hearing the sound of a plane and anti-aircraft fire. That was enough for me, I turned about and bolted indoors where I joined my mother and Mrs Watson in our flat. We could hear bombs exploding, the chatter of machine gun fire and the scream of aircraft engines as three spitfires from Dyce RAF attacked the Heinkel bomber. Many Aberdonians watched the spectacle as the doomed bomber plunged into the partially completed ice rink on South Anderson Drive killing all the crew. We later learned that a number of workers had been killed at Hall Russell's shipyards.

Between the years 1940 and 1943 we had our windows blown out three times. We didn't have an air raid shelter as our flat was in the sunks and it was considered to be safe. Sometimes the whole church building would sway like a ship in a rough sea if the bomb was dropped nearby. The worst raid was the last on Aberdeen in 1943 when a number of Dorniers swept in causing extensive damage to the north of the city and killing 98 people.

When the 'all clear' had sounded that night, I ventured out to have a look around. There seemed to be glass everywhere and I could hear people shuffling through it. The stained glass windows of the church above our flat were hanging down like pieces of tattered cloth. We were very fortunate as the churches on either side of us were badly damaged by bombs. One of the youth organisations was gathered in the hall that night. It must have been an anxious time for the parents until they found out they were unharmed.

Our church hall was one of those earmarked as a rest centre to give shelter to people made homeless through enemy action. Each centre was given a supply of bedding, blankets and emergency rations. Voluntary workers helped to organise the tea and biscuits which the victims got on arrival, many of whom were badly shaken having lost their home and most of their possessions. Next morning they got breakfast and efforts were made to accommodate them elsewhere. There were many anxious moments when frantic relatives came looking for survivors. Some may have been on duty as air raid wardens or the fire service, and when they arrived home they discovered there was only a pile of rubble where their house had been.

Saddest of all were the servicemen who came home on compassionate leave to discover that some of their family had been killed in the raids. In wartime we were inundated with slogans and propaganda to boost our morale on what was known as the Home Front. Paper became a scarce commodity resulting in smaller print and smaller newspapers and magazines. Considerable priority was of course given to the government which included the Board of Trade, the Ministries of Food, Fuel and Agriculture as well as the National Savings Committee. We were urged to save money and to buy National Savings stamps and certificates. The posters screamed the message 'Beware of the Squander Bug', a nasty hairy creature with big ears and sharp teeth, which induced people not to spend their money.

Various new recipes were printed in newspaper and magazines. There are those of us who give a gastronomic shudder at the words 'reconstitute one dried egg'. In spite of the reassurance from the Food Ministry that dried eggs were one of the finest foods that war time rationing had bought us, there was nothing to beat a real fresh egg.

The blackout brought about many hazards and sometime sadly loss of life. All windows and doors had to be covered by curtains, blinds or shutters so that not a chink of light could be seen outside. Even hand torches were hooded and vehicles had headlamps covered showing only slits of light. The passengers on various modes of public transport often had difficulty finding their destination, although the conductor or conductress often called out the name of the street or road to help their disorientated passengers. On the streets a number of black eyes were caused by sudden and violent contact with a lamp post, but mugging was unknown.

If an enemy bomber prowling overhead spotted a light the crew would promptly drop their lethal load in the assumption that where there is light there is life. There was a great increase in the number of weddings at our church during the war years. Many members of the forces came home on a short embarkation leave. This was given before they were posted overseas for an unspecified time. The usual notice for a marriage or proclamation of banns was waived and a much shorter period allowed. Our minister, sometimes accompanied by my father, would announce the bride and groom's name from the church steps thus proclaiming that the couple wished to be married. These weddings were a combination of joy and sadness as the couples knew that their time together was short and their future unknown. I recall one wedding which caused quite a consternation. The groom was a most pleasant and charming Maltese seaman, the bride a local lass and the marriage took place without a hitch. However, sometime later inquiries were made regarding the marriage, it turned out that our charming Maltese was a bigamist as he already had a wife in Malta!

Aberdeen had quite a number of cinemas in the forties, most of which are now long gone. Some of the larger cinemas such as the Capitol on Union Street and the Astoria in Kittybrewster had large elaborately decorated cinema organs which rose from the pits or glided sedately in from the wings. The organist, during the interval, entertained the audience with popular tunes of the times. Sometimes the lyrics were shown on the screen and patrons were invited to join in, which they usually did with gusto. This was before cigarettes carried a government health warning and the air was heavy with smoke. Copious quantities of the haze must have been inhaled by smokers and non smokers alike during these sing songs but no one cared. If an air raid siren blew, warning of a pending air raid, it was shown on the screen. The choice was left to the individual if they wished to leave, but most of the audience remained where they were.

Around the corner from John Knox's Church on Nelson Street was one of the smaller cinemas – the Globe, or the 'Flechy Globbie' as it was sometimes known. As one local wag said you went 'in wi' a jersey and oot wi' a jumper'. However, the risk of being host to a flea didn't deter the patrons one bit. On a Saturday there was usually a serial film for the youngsters which ended in a nail biting moment of excitement. This ensured that everybody returned the next Saturday to follow the further adventures of their hero or heroine.

I was fortunate in having a very happy and secure childhood. The war years were an exciting time for me; although we didn't have a radio my father purchased a number of newspapers and magazines. These I studied in great detail after my father had read them.

I saw very little of my brother Alex as, after evading capture at Dunkirk, he was abroad most of the war. However, my cousin Rosie who was an Air Ambulance Orderly in the WAAFs spent a number of her leaves with us before she too went abroad. I would listen enthralled to her stories of life in the forces wishing that I was of age to enlist. Needless to say, with the fickleness of youth, I never did 'join the colours', but went for the wide open spaces and agriculture instead.

WHEN THERE WAS INNOCENCE

W Gordon Lawrence

Sometimes on days of sunshine as a child I played in the Sandy Hole in the Parish of King Edward in Buchan. The Sandy Hole was the remaining, exposed part of a beach left marooned – a marine terrace – after the glacial period, when new land had erupted from the then sea bed. There during the summer holidays, where once the sea had washed and beat against the beach, I would go for picnics in the afternoon with visiting aunts and cousins to play rounders and French cricket with tennis racquets long past their prime. I played in the way only children can on 'the seashores of endless worlds', as Tagore observed.

On wet afternoons, I sometimes would listen to records on the mechanical gramophone stored in the outhouse – which was called the 'chaumer' – where, long ago, apprentices had slept. The records were all dusty, some were cracked and others had warped in the sun. Dance tunes of the nineteen thirties dominated the small collection, but the one I enjoyed the most was by a Scottish comedian. I can still hear in memory his rousing song that could be played at varying speeds, which made it even more comical, as I experimented with different registers from a lugubrious, leaden *basso profoundo* through to the voice of a demented *castrato*.

> I never work on Mondays,
> Tuesdays that's the same,
> Wednesdays that's a holiday noo,
> Thursdays the weather's tae blame,
> Fridays near the end of the week,
> There's nae use in startin' then,
> An' I'll no get a job on a Setturday noo,
> Till Monday comes again.'

The years were the early War years. In the summer of 1940 I had been sent to stay with my grandparents in Aberdeenshire. Being now their age I marvel at their capacity to take on the raising of a five year old. To my eyes they were very old indeed. My grandmother never substantially changed in appearance for the rest of her life. My grandfather was bald and had been, I subsequently discovered, since his early twenties. Because his head was always covered when outside, I would look at the stunning paleness of his cranium when he was in the house as if it was a different head because it was so vulnerable looking, like a hen's egg shell.

My grandfather was the local 'vricht': joiner, blacksmith, sawyer, house painter and, on rarer occasions, funeral undertaker. Each of these activities had its territory. The biggest was the joinery where all the benches of the men were around the wall. Facing each bench were their tools neatly arranged in racks against the stone wall. Chisels, graded in size and purpose, hung regimented. Tenon, cross cutting, and ripping saws hung above their benches within easy reach. More rarely used bow saws, with their dusty strings which could be tautened by a peg, hung on nails embedded in the wall. Trying, smoothing and jack planes made of wood but increasingly of steel, which were referred to as 'Stanley Planes', were set on a raised bar at the end of the bench to protect their blades. Each bench had a vice in which wood to be planed and chiselled would be set. Tools were the possessions of the joiner and were treated with pride and near reverence, being regularly oiled and sharpened. In their blue dungarees the joiners carried boxwood rulers, spirit levels, and sometimes try squares, in special pockets, along with broad leaded pencils.

A loft over the chaumer where the gramophone sat, was reached by stairs and there, as on the rafters above the workshop, were stored well seasoned planks and boards of ash, oak, elm and mahogany. Some of these, I overheard my grandfather tell a farmer, were to be used for his coffin. The loft was where the swallows nested and the skylights had always to be open to allow them free access. In summer they would be swiftly swooping around the buildings and one day in autumn they would disappear. They were migrating to we knew not where, leaving us earth bound, but aware that come the spring they would reappear as sure as night followed day.

Next door was the machine shop with the circular saws and wood planers powered by a Lister engine. A system of belts and pulleys connected the engine to the machines. Later a more modern Petter engine was installed but it did not have the impressive flywheel of the Lister and was of less interest to me. The Lister had a slower, more deliberate pace and sound whereas the Petter was busy and more petulant sounding.

The machine shop was in use daily. Wood had to be sawn and planed to exact measurement. The joiners never trusted one measurement, always there were two or even three made. The planer produced sharp brittle shavings unlike those the men produced when planing by hand. They were slowly, even languorously, spewed from the plane in long, fresh smelling rolls called 'spells'. A spell could wrap around me like the malevolent serpent in the Garden of Eden.

If I hear the scream of a saw on a summer's day now I am transported across time and space to childhood at Danshillock, King Edward. The sawmill abutted the machine shop and was powered by the same engine. When my grandfather had spent a day sharpening the six foot circular saw I knew that a day in the near future would be set aside for work in the saw mill. This was a day of drama which I watched with excitement and sometimes fear. The yard was full of trees which my grandfather had bought from the neighbouring lairds. Previously, he and I would have walked through their woods, marking the trees he wanted with a chalk mark. Calculations were made in cubic feet and noted by him. The cut trees would be delivered to the yard. From the yard the trees were levered, pushed and rolled by the men with much heaving and grunting onto a moving platform that ran on rollers. The rollers had been made years ago on the turning lathe in the machine shop. There were indentations in them which fitted the wooden runners that were under the platform. It was a perfect train for a child. Once the tree was on the platform it was pushed on the railway of rollers into the saw mill. Then the tree had to be heaved and rolled from the platform across planks to another platform which fed the saw. This platform was divided in two for the most part to allow the saw to engage with the tree trunk. This platform was slowly moved by a hand driven crank.

The danger of a tree falling and injuring someone on its journey from the yard to the saw was real. On each stage of the journey the tree was secured with wedges to prevent it from falling off the rolling platform. I kept a prudent distance from all this. What was more dangerous was the actual sawing. A substantial beech tree sometimes had a greater girth than the size of the saw. Then cuts would be made the length of it with the saw; slowly to allow the saw the power to bite. The dying scream of a protesting saw alternated with its being allowed to free run to regain its momentum to finish the task of cutting. The tree would be rolled over and wedges inserted into the cut and hammered until the tree split. All this required strength, skill and accuracy. After the initial excitement the sawing was a straightforward operation. Planks would emerge from the tree that later would be sawn into boards. My task was to drag away the 'backs' of bark to stack them for firewood.

To witness the transformation of a growing tree, condemned by a chalked cross, from its place in the policies of a laird into planks and boards which were fashioned and planed into objects of daily use – such as a wheelbarrow – was to be initiated into the mechanics and, even, the aesthetics of added value. Although I was not to know till years later, I was witnessing the last of a craftsmanship that stretched back to medieval times.

Once a year the centre of the joinery shop was cleared for the construction of a threshing machine which had been ordered by a farmer. The War years were bringing their own prosperity to the farming community, and machinery was being renewed after the depression years of the 'thirties. I never saw any plans for these threshing machines except pencilled sketches with measurements on a piece of board that was a scrap cutting. Over the weeks the threshing machine would take shape. In its pristine, sweet smelling hull I would play at being a pirate during the evenings when the men had gone home.

It was at this time that the blacksmith's forge would be used. My task was to pump the bellows that brought the fire in the forge to its intense heat. The bellows were six foot or so in diameter and the long handle had to be jumped for to set the bellows blowing. Rods, bolts and iron plates were fashioned in the fire, shaped on the anvil and tempered in a barrel of water. All were fitted to the threshing machine. Finally it was painted in the chosen colour of the farmer, obliterating the pink primer which I had helped to brush on the raw wood.

I wanted to go everywhere with my grandfather. If I thought he was going anywhere I would lurk around the blacksmith's shop where the Wolsley was garaged. It was always referred to by its name, never as the 'car'; and we 'motored' everywhere, never drove. The fourteen horse power Wolsley had brown leather seats and a dignified presence because of its graceful lines. Our greatest speed was thirty miles per hour.

Sometimes we would go to Banff to buy supplies from Lyons the ironmongers. My grandfather had a passion for buying packets of nails, screws, hinges, brackets, tins of paint and drums of putty. My grandfather would have had no concept of contemporary, just-in-time buying strategies, fetching his requirements at the last moment; rather he held a just-in-case policy.

The motoring was for Saturdays and holidays when I was not at school. My grandfather walked me to school on my first day. In the mornings he wore a dungarees, of a pale blue from all their washings, over his suit. It would have been in late summer because he had on his straw hat. The seasons could be marked by his headgear. In winter it was a cap but, later, I knew when summer was coming because on went the straw hat. It was barely a quarter of a mile to school up the main Aberdeen–Banff trunk road. We walked, the two of us, from the house over the bridge to a cluster of buildings comprising the local shop, the farm with the name of Danshillock and the school with its school house, where Mr Arklay the dominie lived. As we passed the shop my grandfather volunteered that he had been born there, pointing to an uninhabited outhouse. I said, 'But that's a wash hoose. You were born in a wash hoose.' He replied sharply that it hadn't been a wash house then.

School was enjoyable because I was usually top of the class. Mr Arklay had welcomed me with a smile announcing to the class that he had taught my uncles and my aunts and that I would be the best. He was an Edinburgh graduate and the twenty-third headmaster since the Reformation. To satisfy his prediction I strove to be the *dux* of the day. The winner for the day received the medal. In truth it was a silver sixpence with a hole bored through it for the ribbon. I had to win the medal otherwise the apprentices, Wullie Sharpe in particular, would not speak to me. Because I was lonely the apprentices were essential to my conversational life. Sonsy, smiling Wullie was my friend and I would spend hours in his company. Once I had teased him too much or done him some mischief, and he took me and plunged me bawling into the rain barrel. My grandfather said that what he had done was quite right and I learned my first lesson in justice.

The winters at school were punctuated by snowstorms. Because I lived so close to school there was no reason why I should miss it. For other children the snow drifts were often so high they had to stay at home. My greatest desire was to have tackety boots, thick woollen stockings and breeches like the other boys. It took a lot of persuading but in the end I had my wish. One cold day my grandmother presented me with a leather helmet that had belonged to one of my uncles. It was a match of Jim Mollinson's and Amy Johnson's helmets ('Amy Johnson in an aer-o-plane!') whose aviation exploits I heard tell of. I went to school through the drifts with my arms outstretched; a solo Spitfire powered by tackety boots.

But school was also in spring and summer and autumn. Daffodils in a clay jug are still for me the most evocative of flower arrangements because their vivid yellow, which one could never capture in crayons or water colours, heralded hope of summer. Snowdrops, tingling white in their purity, set in a glass tumbler on the teacher's desk is a lifelong image. And where else but school would one find catkins slowly burgeoning in a pitcher on the window sill?

In school we talked and wrote in English but outside and at home we spoke Doric. School was therefore a special place with its own language. A *pooch* in the playground was a pocket in the classroom, *brook* was soot, *chave* to work hard, *nowt* were cattle, *lug* an ear, *greet* to cry, *clake* to gossip, *sark* a shirt, and *swack* was to be supple. We *tholed*, or endured, the school with its different language and rituals of forming lines and moving our places in the class to attain the top desk. We wrote and did our sums on slates and kept them clean with our spit. In winter we huddled round the pot bellied stove and in summer dozed to the sound of indolent blue-bottles.

Our family life, too, was governed by rituals. On Sunday my grandfather and I would pace our way to Church. There we sat in the gallery and listened to Mr Selkirk, the minister. At collection time the elders would come round with boxes on the end of long poles into which the penny was dropped. My grandfather would slip me a pandrop before the sermon and I would concentrate on making it last till the end of Mr Selkirk's discourse.

Shovel-hatted Mr Selkirk, a rarely seen figure, lived in the Manse which was a very substantial house surrounded by his glebe. The Manse was by the old Church of Kinedward which was now an ivy-covered ruin. This church at the time of Bishop Elphinstone (1493-1514), had been part of the Abbey of Deer. We worshipped in the new church at the cross roads on the Aberdeen–Banff road. There, as in every village, was the War Memorial listing the dead from the 1914-18 War. Lairds' and cottars' sons were equal in death. Now we were silently wondering whose name would be on it after the War which we were now fighting.

A regular Sunday afternoon outing after Church in the morning and our midday dinner was to visit my great grandmother in Alvah. She died on the first of December, 1940, aged eighty four. She was bedridden and I was terrified of her, for she looked like an old witch with the occasional wisps of hair growing from her cheeks. I would be presented to her, and from the darkness of the box bed a hand would emerge which I had to shake. It was the length of her curling finger nails that revolted me. She was taken care of by my great aunt Isabella who had come home from America on the death of my great-grandfather in 1935 to look after her mother.

They lived on the croft which had the name of Fattahead, sometimes written 'Fattiehead'. The croft was part of the Abercromby estate and was rented by my family from 1862 till 1966 according to the receipts I possess. My great-great-grandfather Charles was the first tenant. He, like his sons after him, drained the land and made it arable. When he died in 1889 an inventory was made of his 'growing crops and moveable effects'. His two acres of oats, two acres of turnips, and two acres of potatoes and 'about 50 stones Hay' were valued at sixteen pounds sterling and ten shillings. His cow, one year old stirk and pig realised thirteen pounds, twelve shillings and six pence. His milk basin, churn, girdle, broom and brush, bed and table linen and other household effects came to seven pounds, one shilling and nine pence, and that included his 'Body Clothes' worth two pounds and five shillings. Altogether, the valuation came to the grand total of thirty nine pounds, ten shillings and six pence.

The annual rent which Charles Lawrence paid in 1863 for Fattahead was two pounds, thirteen shillings and eight pence. My father, in 1966, was paying the trustee of Sir George William Abercromby, Baronet of Birkenbog and Forglen, a rent of two pounds, fourteen shillings and five pence.

As a five-year-old I had little notion of history except that at the croft they were old. Isabella was a plumpish woman who always wore tennis shoes and garments which one knew were from America because of their brightness of colour. Behind all the conversations of these elders there were dramas I knew nothing of till later. My grandfather had two sisters. They both emigrated to America and became, as my grandfather would say, 'Yankees'. They owned rooming houses in Brooklyn, New York and remained spinsters. After the 1914-18 War my grandfather too had wanted to emigrate but my grandmother refused. He not liking to be thwarted said that he would not pay any housekeeping money except for the 'hens meat', which was what he did for the rest of his life. Consequently, they maintained separate bank accounts.

On Sunday afternoons – playing outside the house of the croft of Fattahead because I was too frightened to go inside to the peat laden gloominess – I had no thought of this. Then I had no idea that my family had lived their lives since the end of the eighteenth century in the parish of Alvah and, more particularly, on the two neighbouring properties of Ryland and Fattahead.

The history begins, in the sense that it is as far as I have been able to trace, with a Charles Lawrence of Ryland in Alvah who had a son William born in 1782 who, in turn, fathered Charles born in 1830 who became the tenant of Fattahead. My great great great aunt Elizabeth who was born in 1790 married a John Mitchell of Herodhill which was but a step along the road from Fattahead. None of them seemed to have travelled very far, though my great great uncle John – who was in born in 1863 – moved to Edinburgh only to die there in 1882. There are gaps in the history because the Registrar of Births and Deaths for King Edward parish watered the official ink for a good many years and so the records have faded.

My grandfather was no exception to this rootedness in the environs of his birth, though he had his ambitions. He had established himself in business in his early twenties as a joiner at Brydock, which lies a mile from where he was brought up. Later he took the tenancy of Danshillock from the Craigton Estate, which belonged to the Urquharts, who are descended from Sir Thomas Urquhart, the translator of Rabelais. Born in 1611, Sir Thomas received the rudiments of his education at King Edward school. He was for his contemporaries, 'the fantastic knight with the unbridled imagination'.

My father told me of how the family moved from Brydock to Danshillock. He had the task of driving the two cows, and was able to do so by going across the old Bridge of Alvah on the River Deveron and travelling by Montcoffer to the main Aberdeen–Banff road and thence to Danshillock. The rest of the family had a longer journey, going by the main road through Banff, because the Bridge of Alvah had been unsafe for many years. They were transported by a steam traction engine to which, like a train, were attached bogies and carts. Everything was carried in one move; household effects, machines, timber and all the accoutrements of a country joiner.

In subsequent years my grandfather visited Glasgow for the Empire Exhibition, but otherwise remained grounded in the parishes of Alvah and King Edward with his longest journeys only to Aberdeen. His domain was mainly the farms where he renovated houses, built cattle courts and supplied threshing mills. The names of these farms were part of daily conversation, lilting in their cadences: Easter Montbletton, Foulzie, Balchers, Gorrachie, Castleton, Fortie, Nether Inverichnie, Scatterty, Auchmill and Strocherie.

The parish of King Edward was originally called 'Kinedart' and that was how we pronounced it locally. When life in Feudal times centred round the medieval Church and Castle, the parish of King Edward was important in Scottish affairs. This was because the local Norman Barons were the Comyns – who were the Earls of Buchan – who held great power and lands in Buchan, in England and in southern Scotland at the time King Edward Castle was built by them in the thirteenth century. After Robert the Bruce was crowned at Scone in 1306 he saw it as imperative to have no opposition from powerful Scottish landowners. Consequently, he set out in the year after to defeat the Comyns which he did at the Battle of Barra in 1307. As a consequence, the importance and wealth of the Comyn family declined. And so too did the parish of King Edward.

Such history I did not know then and I was more preoccupied with the present. Of a summer evening my grandfather's friend Crichton, who was in a substantial way of business of manufacturing threshing mills in Turriff, would call and see him. They always sat either outside or in the saw mill. Crichton, I learned later, was something of what was then called a 'ladies man'. He also liked to drink, which my grandfather never did. But they enjoyed each other's company and respected each other. Crichton would tell of his doings. The punch line of one story I remember unerringly. Whatever the circumstances, Crichton had been threatened with a fight by someone in a public house. Short of wind, fat, bespectacled Crichton would have been sorely tried in such a combat. 'But,' Crichton said, 'I had a pound of liver in my pocket so I took it out and threw it in his face.'

We never had visitors except family. The exception was Andrew Forbes of Holm. He always wore tweed knickerbocker suits and carried a walking stick – or knobkerry – because he had spent time as a young man in South Africa with the Scottish Horse. He was a bachelor and had a sister who was a nurse in the hospital in Banff. She was always referred to as 'Sister Mary' though whether for her familial or professional role I was never sure. Andrew Forbes did most of the talking, usually about the conduct of the War which we followed regularly through the news bulletins on the wireless and the newspaper. There was a well rehearsed routine of these evenings. At one point my grandfather would enquire once again, as if he could never get the lesson quite right, just what were the causes of the Boer War. And off Andrew Forbes of Holm would go taking us event by event to the brink of the war. Then he would leave. At times, for I found their adult conversation boring, I would will my grandfather to 'ask for the causes', because that would signal the end of the visit of Andrew Forbes of Holm.

There was a paced, deliberate routine to my grandparents' activities. They had in addition to the joinery business a croft of eight acres or so and their lives centred round these two activities. The work for the croft was mainly done in the evenings. We would have the one field of corn to harvest. This entailed my walking behind my grandfather as he 'redded roads', cutting by scythe a path for the binder, round the perimeter of the field. We then made sheaves, binding them with two bunches of corn stalks knotted together. The thistles were painful to my hands. A local farmer would come with his horse drawn binder to harvest the corn and we followed making tacks, or 'stooks'. As the binder came to the last portion of the crop in the middle of the field, rabbits and hares would make their escape. Harvest days were pleasant because the weather had to be fine, and there was the pleasure of a picnic in the field prepared by my grandmother.

The images of these hairst times lay dormant for forty years to be brought alive again while wandering around an Indian village. A poem came:

Here in Dhunkore
I dander aboot
an' glaik at Indian billies chavvin'
awa' wi' little wee sickles
plookin' shaves o' rice;
jist eneuch tae fill yer han'.
An' it taks me back tae hairsts I've kent
an' words an' mem'ries I thocht I'd tint.

I min' fine, noo, stannin' anaith the sun o' India;
– Fit wye did it nivver shine like 'is on Turra?
There canna be twa suns, can there? –
o' the wye ma gran'faither redded roads,
swooshin' awa' wi' his his souple singin' scythe,
tae mak wye for the Clydesdales an' the binder.
An' the marvellin' een o' a little loon
wid watch, an' lairn wi' thissle jobbit han's
tae mak a rape o' stalks an' bin'
the shaves an' stook 'em on the palin'.

I min' fine noo, lis'enin' tae birds like faerlies,

an' watchin' ra' reid ersed monkeys
climmin the banyan trees,
o' a' the dominies 'at thrashed fit little lairnin'
took me on the wye tae fit wid ca'd a 'Profession'.
– Fit wye wis there sae little lovin'
in the skules o' Aiberdeen?

Noo, fin I'm a bit aul'er a mannie,
an' ma lair in Alvah's aul' kirkyard
is comin' jist 'at bittie closer,
I think tae masel, it mibbe wid a bin better
jist tae a bin a jiner like my faither
or a crafter like mither's faither.

Na, na, I've bin gi'en a chice
a' throu' ithers sacrifice
tae chav an' mak ees o' ma min';
tae try an' mak sma' shaves
o' fit may be the truth o' 't.
Bit mibbe noo, 'ears ahin the time
fin I thocht I kent aathin',
I'll lairn anaith 'at same sun
again tae see the warld o' men
wi' the marvellin' een o' a little loon.

Time, territory and tasks on a daily basis were structured by the rhythms of my grandparents' life. Their lives were full of daily purpose: working in the business, on the croft, around the house, in the garden. Effortlessly my life mirrored a little of their tasks. Each evening I would drive the two cows from the field to the byre for milking, would do my homework in term time and go to bed at nine – in winter with my hot water 'pig', and in the summer by the light of the long northern nights.

Within the pattern of my grandparents' life I was free to do what I wanted apart from activities which were obviously dangerous. The concept of time and territory were internalised without effort. At twelve o'clock my grandmother would blow a whistle which meant dinner time.

Its sound carried quite a distance in the quiet of the country before the days of intensive mechanisation and regular traffic on the roads. Since my grandmother was an excellent cook and I was always hungry I was promptly at the table.

I too had space and time for my activities. Above the paint shed there was a loft reached by wooden stairs. The sole cobwebbed window on the gable end looked onto the wood that bordered the stream. There I would spend wet afternoons. From the time of my younger uncles there was a pile of *The Modern Boy* magazines. These I read and re-read – and for a few years pronounced in my head the word 'scientist' as 'skientist'. The loft became my territory by tacit agreement. It was never visited by anyone else. If I was wanted for something I would be called from the bottom of the stairs. There I stayed happily for hours, content with my own company. Then I learned the tranquillity that comes from the capacity to be alone. The glowing sense of security and cosiness and the serene feelings I would have on a wet afternoon as I read *The Modern Boy* and listened to the tintinnabulation of the rain on the corrugated iron roof comes back occasionally when I experience a storm.

The stream that I could see from the window of the paint shed loft was small but deeply set between two wooded banks. Great beech trees gave a shade that was always cool in the heat of summer. From a solid branch on one of these beech trees an uncle had suspended a swing for me. It had long ropes which made for frightening swoops through the air that made me feel nauseous on occasion. The stream was famous because, before there was a bridge, the hated Duke of Cumberland pursuing the Jacobites after the 1745 Rebellion had got stuck in the bank with his heavy guns. The deep scars were still there underneath the matted brambles and ferns.

Playthings, except for a Meccano set, were few but I had all the richness of the natural objects of the joinery and the croft to enjoy. New paling posts were stacked in triangles, one on top of the other, to allow them to season. They made perfect forts and, as the war years proceeded with their intensified military images, they became tanks and bunkers. There was always the sawmill railway to ride up and down on. There were places to explore.

In time I mastered my aunt's discarded bicycle which had no cross bar and was easy to ride. Round and round the close I pedalled, ever more quickly, until the inevitable crash, torn knee and tears. In time I became more adventurous and the world extended as far as I could travel on my bike. Later, I visited my great uncle Duncan Wyness who was the head gamekeeper for Major Robert Abercromby at Dunlugas. It was a stilted visit for I recall Uncle Duncan as a taciturn man, but my great aunt had a twinkling quality.

Although my visit was unannounced they made an effort to make it interesting. It was a new world for me. There in the garage were shooting brakes with varnished wooden bodies and Rover cars parked all the year until Major Robert came home to shoot and fish. The housekeeper showed me over the mansion house. I learnt of drawing rooms, dining rooms, libraries and gun rooms. I was surprised that the laird had a separate bedroom from his wife and had a room just for dressing.

Uncle Duncan's sister was my grandmother on my mother's side. The contrast between the two sets of grandparents was so remarkable it could be recognised by a child. My mother's parents lived in New Byth where they had a croft attached to their house in the village. The houses were built of sandstone blocks of an earthy, red colour. Some important houses had slate roofs, a dwindling number were thatched. An increasing number of householders were replacing the thatch with corrugated iron roofs, which rusted to match the stone but gave the village a shanty town air.

If life at Danshillock was always clean and comfortable, New Byth was run down and poor. It had, however, its own riches in that my grandmother was a remarkable story teller. She and I would spend the day rarely moving from the fireside while she told me about the great castles in which my grandfather and she had served. The questions were of the nature: 'What was it like at Delgaty Castle?' And she would launch into an account of the family and the furnishing of the castle, thus giving me a sense of what it might be like to live in such grandeur with glimpses of the occupant's eccentricities. 'They used to send their sons to Eton on the train with a luggage label round their necks.'

My maternal grandparents lived their lives in one room in which they ate, slept and were irritable with each other. On the bottom floor of the house were two more rooms. One was furnished as a best room with a memorable pair of cast iron, white painted lurchers standing sentinel by the never used fireplace. Off it there was a bedroom. The upstairs of the house had three empty rooms except one where a stuffed mallard duck kept vigil silently and blindly through the years.

All the cooking was done on the peat fire which had a 'swingle tree' on which kettles and pots would be hung. We drank a lot of tea and often had eggs. I dreaded having to go to search for eggs. The henhouse was dark and dank and the nests would often be presided over by some wily hen who would painfully peck the back of my hand. To be sent for eggs from the duck house (the 'dyeuks hoose') was more frightening. The floor was of slimy mud which had to be negotiated without slipping to reach the nests. If a peck from the hen is painful the nip from a duck is worse.

The eggs were boiled in the same kettle from which the tea was made. My grandmother never washed the eggs and I timidly enquired if it would not be a bad idea to do so, holding in mind the standards of Danshillock. Her reply was to the effect that it made the tea taste better. But she had a grace and a sensibility that my more well-off paternal grandmother did not have. Arranged on her dresser in the kitchen was a collection of beautiful milk jugs which had originally had their utilitarian uses but now were there for their colourfulness and memories of a better life.

My New Byth grandfather had no car but something even better: a gig and a 'shelt'. The gig had shining brass lamps and in its heyday would have been an elegant equipage. No-one in the village had anything like it. Occasionally, he and I would ride to the mill with sacks of corn to have them ground. A gig with a sedately stepping pony gives the passenger a sense of airiness with a feeling that the countryside is there to be slowly regarded and appreciated.

Occasionally there would be an air raid alert. Mr Buchan the tailor, with a tin helmet for his warden role, would alert us by blowing a whistle while bicycling up the street. My grandmother took these raids seriously and I would be placed in a musty, paraffin smelling cupboard under the stairs. She would never come with me and the fears of that confined space were more real than any destruction any bomb could bring. In fact I would have welcomed a bomb just to get out of it.

Childhood then, both at New Byth and Danshillock, was illuminated by paraffin oil lamps and candles and, sometimes in the main living rooms, by an angrily hissing Tilley lamp with its fragile mantle. I preferred the large oil lamps with their gentle bathing of light on the pages of the book I would be reading. Candles were more frightening because of the deep, palpable, flickering shadows they revealed. The small oil lamp I had for going to bed was more benign. That soft glow and velvet shadows have been banished to history.

Danshillock was a Presbyterian, pragmatic household which gave little credence to the imagination. I doubt if my grandfather ever read anything except the local newspapers and the *Daily Express* for he liked Rupert the Bear. Usually he would ask me if I had seen what Rupert was up to today. My grandmother read the *People's Friend* which I surreptitiously read for many years too because it was the only literature available. Fiction for me was shaped by Annie S. Swan – dropped handkerchiefs in Waverley Gardens always brought a handsome man into the heroine's life. Faintly guilty I would turn the pages of the mail-order catalogues to have vaguely exciting feelings as I looked at the substantial ladies modelling corsets.

Life was lived rhythmically with the seasons. Most afternoons in summer my grandmother would be in the garden where all the vegetables we ate were grown: her pride was the large strawberry beds she maintained. The beds were protected by old herring fishing nets which would be renewed every few years. The nets covered a construction of three foot high posts and rails that allowed my grandmother to tend her strawberries and keep them safe from the birds. She bent from the waist and never bent her knees so I have memories of her angular shape. The strawberry beds were prohibited to me. On an afternoon after dinner when I knew they both would be having naps I would poach the beds with a beating heart, ease my hand under the nets, cull and eat strawberries. I was always careful to replace the nets so that no bird could enter. Years later, crawling on some part of Salisbury Plain, hugging the ground, and moving on my elbows and knees to take part in yet another tedious attack as part of my officer training, I recalled stalking strawberries on a summer's afternoon.

The garden was well stocked with apple trees, plum trees, raspberries, gooseberries, black and red currants. The window of my bedroom overlooked the garden. In a corner of the garden roses grew abundantly beside a disused privy. They were heavily scented from their pink and red velvety, cabbage-like heads. They were voluptuous, but once picked their petals would fall and the rose would be no more; which always made me feel tinges of what I came to know as sadness.

A hawthorn hedge which had to be trimmed enclosed the garden. Gradually I was initiated into this task which I enjoyed. A sword with an extra wooden handle bolted to it was used for this cutting. To stand on a box to give height and slash the tough hedge with a real sword was to fight all the battles of history on a summer's afternoon. If Prince Charles had fought with my resolve we would have a Jacobite king on the throne for sure.

My grandfather spent some afternoons in his office. This was a small room just off the sitting room at the front of the house where, in winter, we spent our evenings. Across the hall from there was another room, the best room, with its piano and little used furniture where my aunt did her courting. My grandfather's office I never entered except, which was rare, by explicit invitation. On my own I would look at it by standing on the floor of the little sitting room and bending my body to see what I could. His pencils were always arranged in jars, a habit I keep to this day. There would be plans of steadings and houses lying around. There he 'did his books' in the phrase of the time. I must never disturb him as he engaged in this activity. I was, however, very curious as to what he did in his office. What was the meaning of 'doing the books?' One afternoon I decided to find out. Across the window of the office grew the espaliered branches of a plum tree. Carefully I climbed up it and stretched myself along the strongest looking branch. There he was sitting at his desk sleeping. I watched for some time taking in all the details of the room from the bird's eye viewpoint. Then he woke up and looked straight at me. I was so astonished I fell off the branch which caused him to laugh.

That he was not very assiduous in doing the books came out when he died. There may still be standing some cattle courts and steadings on the farms of the parish of King Edward and its neighbours that my grandfather was never paid for. This was partly because he did not render his accounts as rigorously as he might. When he died the solicitor collected about four and a half thousand pounds in outstanding accounts. It also came out that my grandfather did not pay personal income tax because he did not agree with the principles of it.

At the same time he had a kind of contempt for money. His habit, it was discovered after his death, was to empty his pockets of cash before he went to the bank to draw money for the men's wages. This he did into the bottom drawers of his dressing table. When he died, the twenty to thirty years collection of groats (four penny pieces), pennies and shillings – even white five pound notes – were counted and hoarded. It was the final gesture; the last grandiose *pourboire* of my grandfather to posterity.

I suspect that his inability to have farmers pay their bills was more to do with the nature of relationships between farmers and the likes of my grandfather at the time. There was a tolerance of indebtedness because they had all come out of the 1930's recession and there might have been the willingness to pay but there was little cash in the economy. It was the War that brought prosperity. When a farmer did come to pay his bill he was offered a dram of whisky and, probably, he asked for a 'luck penny' as well to reduce his account. My grandfather never drank to my knowledge and so a bottle of whisky could last a long time. His custom was to buy a new one when it was about a third of the bottle down. When he died there was a cupboard laden with bottles of whisky two thirds full.

There were swings of mood to the life also. My grandmother was very bad-tempered, but only at set, predictable times. On a weekly basis there was the Monday washing. This was done in an outhouse next to the kitchen. She had a manual washing machine. I can still see her thrusting the handle backwards and forwards. But they were brief glimpses, swift glances through the door, as I saw her face contorted with effort. Then the clothes went through a wringer. Oh! the fear of trapping fingers in those rollers still lingers to this day. Monday was the worst day of the week because for dinner we had 'stovies', which is potatoes mixed with meat and cooked in a pot with some onions, with plain semolina pudding to follow.

Most mornings she was bad-tempered. After dinner there was a change. In the morning I never went near the kitchen after breakfast. After we had eaten at midday and after the tranquillity for 'swarging' – the time for a nap and digestion – she would settle down in the kitchen on a horsehair chaise longue by the window to do her darning and sewing. The sun would be coming in from the small window overlooking the garden. The light was perfect for sewing and, at the same time, illuminated her face and transformed her countenance. Sometimes I would steal on tiptoe into the kitchen in the quiet of the afternoon, disturbed only by the sound of browsing hens and desultory flies, just to look at her from the chair next to the door, but poised ready for escape. In the evenings she was calm except for a short period after milking time when she retired to her pantry to separate the milk, which was done by a machine that rang a bell. The pantry, which was quite a big room, was off the kitchen and was uniquely her preserve. In phantasy no male entered this temple of purity devoted to milk products.

Between the two of them there would be touching moments of which I was the sole witness. Often after dinner my grandmother would offer my grandfather a cigarette. He would take it gingerly from the packet as if he had never seen such an artefact before, light it with a spill, and, holding it between his thumb and first finger with the others delicately crooked, regard it as if it was to explode. He would smoke a little and say that was enough for now. That was the nearest I saw affection between them. They never touched each other and I was never kissed by either.

My grandmother's bad temper had resulted in all the implements for dealing with the stove being broken as she had thrown them down with impatience. The family members have floated various explanations for her temperament. She had, we agree, a hard childhood. She was born on the eleventh of November in 1882 to Samuel Horn and Jane Wilson who were married at Drumblade in 1879 and she was baptised Jane Gordon Watt. The earliest ancestor we can find for her was a James Horn who married Elizabeth Barron in 1795 at Drumblade near Huntly. My grandmother had three elder sisters. One married Sandison the Souter (shoemaker) of Low Street, Banff. He was a quiet man but she was always talking, setting asway her jet jewellery, which gave her a sinister look despite her smiles. Another sister was a spinster who had the Post Office and shop at Nigg, on the south side of Aberdeen, and is remembered for her very thick pebble lensed spectacles. A third was married to a farmer called Peddie who farmed at Newmacher.

The story was that my grandmother was given away by her parents to her mother's younger sister Mary who was married to a James Macgregor. He was a farm servant at the time of his marriage in 1876 but subsequently a carter. It can be imagined that my grandmother must have felt the rejection, for even to my eyes the other three sisters seemed to have a bond that my grandmother was not a part of. The fact that she could remember being taken away by Jimmie Macgregor and had memories of her own family made the adoption all the more wrenching. The first son of my grandparents, who was subsequently legitimated by their marriage but who died at the age of two, was James Macgregor Lawrence so my grandmother must have had feelings towards her adopted father. We can only assume that she was given away to her aunt and uncle because of the poverty of Samuel Horn, her father.

We were living in 'War Time' and the words were pronounced with the seriousness they deserved. I was aware of War at least twice a day when we listened to the wireless news bulletins. I was involved because of my favourite Uncle called Sam. He had been at Dunkirk and I remember him being on leave because we shared the same bedroom and I was no longer scared of the dark and the rats in the walls. He was captured at the fall of Singapore and became a Japanese prisoner. For the remainder of my childhood he was a permanent shadow-presence in the family's life. Whatever my grandparents thought of his privations was never voiced. We were allowed to send postcards which had to be typed and of no more than twenty seven words, or some such number. Much time was spent agonising over the best formulation of the message for these cards. They were committed to the post. At the end of the War they were returned, never having been delivered by the Japanese. But this was the tragic side of War. It was much more hilarious on a daily basis. Of a summer's evening we would go and watch the Local Defence Volunteers (LDV) practice their drill and the shooting of rifles. Later they became the Home Guard and had uniforms to replace the sleeve band of the former LDV. We expressed considered and considerable misgivings about their abilities.

The realities of War, however, were at a safe distance. We read about bombing raids, offensives, the Battle of Britain and all the dreadfulness of man's inhumanity. Within five years we were to accommodate German and Italian prisoners of war, encounter displaced persons from Estonia, Latvia, Lithuania and Poland, learn of the concentration camps and the Holocaust, see a Europe divided into Blocs which were to last near fifty years, and live in a world where there was always a war or famine somewhere.

The feeling of innocence began to erode as I grew to recognise more of what was happening in the world of my elders. The recognition that there could be both love and hate, malice and charity, good and evil complicated what had seemed to be an understandable world. I became aware of feelings of guilt and the necessity for reparation; sensed loss and the kind of depression children can have. But, at the same time, I experienced affection and love though I could not have named these feelings with any sureness for we of Buchan are undemonstrative in our affections.

These transitions in myself were paralleled by other greater changes that perceptibly began to steal across our landscape in the years following 1939. Then occurred the beginnings of a transformation in the rural routine as horses were replaced by tractors and combine harvesters which marched through the ripened corn. Mechanical potato diggers and four furrow tractor ploughs speeded processes that had been labour intensive since Neolithic times. The traditional muck that had fed our fields for generations increasingly was replaced by fertilisers from sacks. Although we did not know it these transformations were to lead to a prosperity that would have us all in the plenitude and pathos of the consumer society.

Knowledge of the bigger world extended as uncles on leave would describe life in India, Burma and, what was then, Siam, for I was a curious child. Looking in my atlas at the kitchen table to find these countries I was watched from a steel engraving, which hung above the elaborate, mahogany dresser, by an imperious Sir Colin Campbell. He was forever heroically transfixed on his horse with flaring nostrils, as he engaged in some Empire battle. History was on the wall but was also in the making. To be sure, it was a way of life that is now lost and which, like innocence, never can be regained except as myth.

Thirty odd years after these events I was visited by a dream on the eve of beginning my psychoanalysis, dramatically bringing the felt truth of the meaning of my childhood. The scene is of a snow covered landscape, like the Hungarian Plain. The light is disappearing for it is late afternoon. On the horizon is a hamlet. Smoke rises from the chimney. I am part of a small crowd of people, all unknown, at the funeral of a nameless baby. The mourners are from the hamlet but in the dream no-one could be identified as a parent or relative. All seem to be present out of a sense of duty. The priest commits the small coffin to the grave which the two sextons begin to fill with earth. We all begin to walk towards the houses on the horizon, plodding through the snow, burdened by boots, long coats of fur or heavy cloth, and with our heads shrouded.

I am the last to leave. I watch the grave diggers at their task of shovelling the frozen soil on to the coffin. I too begin to walk away to join the retreating mourners ahead of me. In the still silence with which only snow can blanket a landscape I think I hear a baby crying. I stop walking and hold my breath. It's true: it is a baby's cry. I run after the disappearing mourners, shouting, 'The baby is alive. Can't you hear it crying?' They pay no attention as, with heads bowed, they concentrate on plodding through the snow. I run as best as I can through the snow, high stepping to clear its height. I trip on the skirts of my coat, fall often, but struggle on till I reach the nearest mourner. I shout that the baby is alive. He or she, for the face is wrapped against the cold, shrugs me off.

I turn back and run to reach the grave, easily identifiable because of the fresh earth. The sextons have gone with their shovels. I can still hear the baby crying as I start to dig with my bare hands, I throw aside lumps of frozen earth, scrabble at the loose soil, murmuring in response to the cries, 'It's all right, I will get you out.' I dig frenziedly with bleeding fingers but the dream does not reveal if the baby is alive or not.

What I am grateful for were the years at King Edward. They have stood throughout the vicissitudes of life as a symbolic seashore of endless worlds.

DRAMAS OF CHILDHOOD

Marion P Swogger

My earliest memory is being a four-year-old at Blackhall Castle, Banchory, to where most of St Margaret's School in Aberdeen had been evacuated. It was the weekend and my parents were visiting me; I was promising them that the next weekend, if they brought my new black velour winter hat, I would try very hard *not* to cry when they arrived and left. I managed to keep the first part of the promise. I wasn't desperately unhappy; soon there were at least two other girls my own age and later on my brother joined me for a few months and that made an incredible difference to me. It made us grow very close. I remember my fifth birthday; he and another boy came into my dormitory and gave me all their toy cars to play with. Unfortunately, I had to give them all back at breakfast time, but it was still the best birthday present I ever received. I can remember only one example of thoughtless cruelty: an exasperated housekeeper (I had probably been asking too many questions at the wrong time) locked me in a cupboard next to the dormitory. I can still remember the awful fear and claustrophobia of being in that dark small space, and also my self-righteous indignation. I wasn't unhappy. I have memories of the older girls being carelessly kind – but I was very shy and nervous; I couldn't yet say my 'Rs' and my 'Ss' so answering questions in class was an agony of embarrassment for me. My truly happy moments came on the two-mile walks from the bus stop up the drive, walking on my own, looking at the trees and the wild flowers, but most of all at the River Dee, becoming familiar with certain groups of stones and watching the water rush or slide over them.

I can remember feeling strange, on my return home after eighteen months; I was so happy I rushed up the stairs so I could bump down on them on my bottom (a coming-home ritual) but I felt somehow as if I didn't belong. This feeling could only have lasted a few months, but it was very scary, and its negative aspect, almost dislike, was directed at my mother. My mother was working in my father's shop; in fact, my mother had never *not* worked; she went out to work at the age of eleven and didn't stop until she was seventy. These were not easy years for her; she was constantly concerned about her family, all of whom were in London, and she was always in a state of extreme nervous tension because of my father's health. Coping with a strong-willed, antagonistic five-year-old who never stopped asking 'Why?' was an additional strain that remained an undercurrent in our relationship until my twenties. She wanted a well behaved, conventional daughter who would be like 'Them' – whoever 'They' were. As the months passed, the wariness receded and she would entertain me with stories of her family and childhood. When it was decided that she should visit her family, I went with her.

I entered a completely new world; it wasn't just the greenness and the lushness of the landscape and the differences in the architecture, it was the *family*. There were warm, loving grandparents; huge friendly uncles who hugged and kissed me; pretty young aunts with *curls* who giggled and smiled and spoilt me rotten. It was warmth and gaiety and it produced a tug in me between my two halves, Scottish and English. Soon it was to be reinforced by my introduction to two very long-lasting influences on me.

I remember trailing home from school one day and announcing that we could have 'elocution lessons', whatever they were. My father was immediately enthusiastic; I would learn to speak 'properly'. As I could now say my 'Rs' and 'Ss' I didn't see the need to learn any more, but I didn't have any choice. My first lesson was extraordinary. The teacher was quite unlike anyone I had ever seen or heard before. She had been an actress (an *actress*!). She had dyed red hair, a gravelly voice, chain-smoked through the lessons and, I suspect, very often had a severe hangover. She very quickly made it clear that we weren't going to study children's poetry; we were going to study Shakespeare and I was going to act *all* parts. I must have been about seven, and suddenly this magical world opened before me; if I was Puck or Oberon, I was also Viola, Juliet, Portia, Marc Anthony – even Richard III. My parents had a *Complete Works of Shakespeare* and I devoured it. It was literally my daily companion from then on throughout my teenage years. Before this, my favourite reading had been *Pears Encyclopedia*. I know that sounds ridiculous but I *loved* reading about different cultures and peoples. I was already totally absorbed by reading, mainly history. The first history book I remember was a 'Boys' Brigade' prize of my father's about Robert the Bruce: not only did he become an instant hero, but also there was a wonderfully gruesome depiction of Bruce murdering the Red Comyn, with his sword actually spearing the Comyn's body. I used to chase my brother round the dining-room table, brandishing the ghastly image – a revenge for his three years' distance in age and general male superiority. For there was a definite dichotomy in practice in our household between the theories espoused (Vera Brittain was a great heroine of my father) and the actual daily practices.

Almost about the same time as my discovery of Shakespeare was my discovery that there could be an attraction to religion. Of course we had a certain amount of religious instruction at home, which tended to be of the 'Gentle Jesus, meek and mild,' variety – perhaps my mother's appeal to what she hoped were some gentler qualities in my nature. I could see no connection between this and what went on in our church every Sunday. The over two-mile walk was always taken by the exact same route ('Why can't we go by another way?'). I remember nothing of the service but the sermons. The minister was an Ulster Presbyterian and there was never, ever, any mention of Christ or the Holy Spirit. The texts were always based on the Old Testament – on some dreadful denunciations by a prophet or some obscure battle – to which I hardly listened and understood not a word; but what lent a horrible fascination to these utterly incomprehensible proceedings was that, as he proceeded, the minister's voice got louder and louder and his face got redder and redder until I was sure that, one Sunday, he would literally explode right there in the pulpit.

One Easter Sunday, my mother must have been feeling particularly homesick, because she decided to take my brother Gordon and me to the Easter Service at St Andrew's Episcopal Cathedral. I shall never forget my first sight of a processional: the cross, the candles, the robes, the magnificently joyful sound of 'Hail Thee Festival Day', and as the service proceeded, the beautiful cadences of Cranmer's liturgy. Naturally, too, I was entranced by the decor. I had no knowledge of ecclesiastical architecture, so I saw nothing incongruous about the ceiling being decorated with the badges of all the States of America, and the rather gaudy and flamboyant altar provided me with all the colour and drama I so wanted. My brother became a choirboy and for two years I was able to satisfy some need (artistic? spiritual?) and I knew that when I could, I would return. What I didn't realise then was that I would never shake off the legacy of Calvinism. The end of the war seemed also to signal the end of the severe Calvinism as preached in our home – we went on car-rides, we went on picnics, we could read anything we wanted to on a Sunday, everything became immeasurably lighter in approach and content. The double legacy would always be there, though – hard work and guilt.

What kind of memories do I have of sights and sounds and atmosphere? First the COLD. Getting dressed under the bed clothes in the morning, with the frost an inch deep on the inside of the window panes. Bringing in the washing, stiff with frost. Mother sitting me up on the kitchen table to pull off my wellingtons in the winter, and the backs of my knees being raw and rubbed. The misery of the chilblains all over my hands and feet. Secondly, the *darkness.* On Saturday, my brother and I would have lunch with our next door neighbour and then in the mid-afternoon when it was already becoming dark, we would make our way to my father's shop in George Street. Clinging to my brother, trudging along beside him with that ghastly gas mask always present. It isn't just the crowds, it's the darkness I remember.

The train journeys to and from London: soot everywhere, and smoke, and the corridors packed with soldiers; and we spent the whole journey sitting propped up in the corridor. My mother would fidget about the ration books and try to explain them to me, but she always managed somehow and we were certainly never hungry; the only thing I did want to know was what a banana tasted like. Then – it was early 1945 – we received a food package from the US and in it, my mother proudly announced, were bananas. But they didn't *look* like bananas and they had to be heated up under the grill and they didn't taste right at all! I moped, blamed the Americans, and had to wait at least another couple of years. I have no feelings of deprivation, indeed I wasn't deprived, and I would feel shame at the bare-footed tinkers who would occasionally come selling things around our street.

No cars meant that the Avenue could become our playground and we were able to walk anywhere without fear. I loved playing hide and seek amongst the coat and suit racks in the upstairs of my father's shop and when customers came, hurriedly sliding them back into place on the shiny linoleum floor; and playing with the boxes in the musty store room and with his typewriter in his office. I usually tagged along after my brother, and there would be wonderfully imaginative games in Johnson Gardens, and occasionally my mother would take us blackberrying up at Hazlehead golf course. In a way, so much of one's routine was dictated by family tasks: my favourite was the annual washing of the blankets in the bath tub, when I got to stomp up and down with fairly wild abandon in the warm, soapy water.

Two sounds dominate my memory: first, the hissing and puffing of the steam engine getting ready to leave with the train for Edinburgh. It's a miserable, rainy Sunday afternoon and we're there, as we were every three months, to see my father off on his visit to his specialist in Edinburgh for his necessary examination and treatment. We're all edgy and tearful as my mother has conveyed to us her unbearable fear that one day he won't return. The journey home seems endless as does the evening; we all huddle together Sunday and Monday night in our parents' bedroom where Gordon and I push and shove and backbite. Tuesday afternoon comes and I rush as fast as I can down Viewfield Road and along the Avenue; is he here? Yes, white and very tired and drawn, but back with us once again. In a few days he'll be his usual outspoken, argumentative, graceful and handsome self. Hardly anyone, meeting him, would guess his daily pain, the humiliation his body gives him. But we know, and the fear of death is always there.

War and death – these seemed to me as a child terrifyingly real. My father, because of his experiences in the First World War, was obsessed with the sacrifices of war. We knew by heart his story: the early death of his mother and youngest brother at the same time; his subsequent unhappiness and naïve belief in the glory and righteousness of the war which led him to lie about his age so he could enter the army; the terrible battle of Baupaume where, all the officers dead, he led the final charge of the small remnant of Gordon Highlanders and was himself left for dead. At night-time, there was an 'all clear,' so the opposing armies could search for their wounded, and a friend of my father's found him and carried him back to safety: nineteen years old, shot to pieces, temporarily blinded for two years. What must have sustained him – as well as the devoted nursing he received – was his iron will and determination to have a life, to try and do and be like other men, and his deep, simple religious faith. But I don't think a single day of our lives passed without his thundering about the wickedness of war. He became an outspoken pacifist and this certainly set us apart during the Second World War. His extremely outspoken views alienated most of his friends (and incidentally made us squirm with embarrassment on the trams, in the street, and outside the church). It certainly did not make life easier for my more conventional and non-confrontational mother.

However, his views did not prevent him from becoming, as I teased him later, an extremely active pacifist. Naturally he immediately volunteered for the Home Guard, and we would huddle together in the evenings when he was on duty, waiting for his return – and amazingly, for his gossip! There was an extremely attractive young music teacher in his group – my father always had an eye, if only for the looking, for a 'bonny lassie.' She obviously added a much needed brightness to waiting for the air raid warnings and much to our delight it became obvious that a romance was developing between her and a distinguished artist. My mother and father always talked quite freely in front of us, which could occasionally have embarrassing consequences, because I never knew what I should or should not repeat. Fortunately in this case any gaffes were forgiven, and my growing intellectual horizons were widened considerably thanks to Jackson's treating my 'Why?' questions perfectly seriously.

More exciting than this were the strangers who appeared from time to time at our tea-table. My father was part of a network which was set up to help men escaping from Norway. My father would receive a message that a package had been delivered, he would then outfit the man completely (for obviously they came with nothing) and he and others would provide some necessary money. Then the escapee usually came to high tea with us before my father put him on the train for London. This was an activity we were warned strictly never to talk about, and I was too awestruck by the danger – and the adventure – of it all to say anything to anyone. My mother loved these occasions, and was full of warmth and hospitality: I love to know that right up to the time of her death she was still in correspondence with one of these families. It is good to recall the closeness of family, the fellowship of strangers; we knew how lucky we were in comparison with so many other people.

The worst moments for me were when the air raid sirens started to wail, for I had a dreadful fear of bombs. This fear actually lessened after the night that a bomb aimed for the nursing home at the end of the road (mistakenly identified as an industrial building) missed its target and went down Rubislaw Quarry. Even as children we could sense the feeling of a miracle and comprehend in a little way the adults' more immediate understanding of those 'down South.' There was, however, renewed despair with the advent of the 'flying bombs'; my mother went down to London and brought back my grandparents. I had thought this would be wonderful, but I became aware – perhaps for the first time – of the complexity of human relations when I went into the lounge one Sunday afternoon to find my mother crying. Upset by *her* upset, I asked what the matter was. She had thought that Granny and she would spend a cosy afternoon chatting together, but Granny preferred to stay in her own room writing letters to my aunts; poor soul, she was lonely for the daughters and son that she had lived with and knew so well, whereas this daughter whom she had seen so seldom was like a stranger, and she was unhappy in unfamiliar surroundings. Probably for the first time in my life, I found myself actually comforting my mother, empathising with her, but also trying to explain my Granny's feelings. I was nearly nine. I was growing up.

I don't think I had any awareness of class consciousness until I was about ten or eleven. When I started at St Margaret's in Aberdeen (a remnant of the school had remained there) there were only two other girls in Prep 1. I was very wary and shy that first day when I met them; they were startlingly beautiful little girls: Ann had true platinum hair and vivid blue eyes; Dorothy had big brown eyes and thick, thick long brown hair. They were already fast friends, and could easily have ganged up on me. For the next two years there were just the three of us and I can't remember a single example of bad humour or cross words. We worked together, we played together; favourite time was Friday afternoon when we were allowed to act out a poem, of necessity doubling or tripling our roles. I can visualise even now our spirited rendition of 'Sir Patrick Spens' and our wobbly-voiced singing and acting 'In the Bleak Mid-Winter.' Our teachers were warm and supportive and we almost resented it when our class grew in numbers. We played together in the holidays, usually at Ann's house, as she had a live-in Nanny/housekeeper.

They lived in large houses, I lived in a small house; the difference meant nothing to me. The only thing I was envious of was that Ann's house had a *library*. What bliss, I thought, to have one's very own library and to be able to sit in peace all afternoon and read. When I unexpectedly remarked on this to my mother, she merely sniffed and unfortunately didn't point out that the mothers of both of my friends held very responsible volunteer positions. Later on, I became aware that my mother had very mixed feelings about volunteer work; for her it suggested upper-class patronage. Being southern English, she was herself acutely class-conscious, often unpleasantly so; whereas my father was absolutely devoid of it and was completely at ease with everyone. This made him much more interesting and relaxing company, especially once the war was over. I don't remember any snobbery at school at all; girls of very varied backgrounds went to it, and the school prided itself on its strongly feminist heritage. I never questioned my being sent there, and it wasn't until I went up to University that I found myself being accused of being snobbish and elitist. Of course by then I could see why, but I think the idea would have bewildered my father. He was, after all, a convinced supporter of the Labour Party, and naturally an outspoken one. He was, I suppose, a Fabian Socialist; like Attlee, he had never read Marx. Politics was a favourite topic of discussion in our house, and so naturally the General Election of 1945 was eagerly anticipated. We were having our first holiday, staying at a little boarding house in Crathie. On the day the first results were being announced on the radio, most of the guests went off to climb Lochnagar, leaving my mother and myself and two little old ladies, who very kindly invited us up to their room to listen to their radio. Their room was dominated by a four-poster bed which enchanted me, as I'd never seen one before, and they very kindly gave me permission to play on it. As the results were announced, they became more and more agitated, indeed distraught, and my mother had a hard time soothing them while discreetly hiding her own delight. Every so often one of them would whisper nervously, 'What will they do to the Royal Family? They won't do away with them, will they? There won't be a revolution?' I had the grace to feel sorry for them, but how could I understand? At the age of nine, all I knew was that *our* side had won, that there would be a National Health Service, whatever that might be, and that in some obscure way Gandhi also had won – he was one of my father's heroes. I didn't expect that somehow it would seem even COLDER for the next three years, but I did start taking more interest in contemporary history instead of being completely immersed in gods and goddesses and myths and the Middle Ages. In the next few years I also became aware that my father being Labour (and therefore I being Labour too) was distinctly unusual amongst fellow parents and friends, and I would begin to feel the pressure of conformity. But that lay in the future. For me, at the age of nine, the darkness and the accompanying fear and dread had gone; we were all safe and secure; I knew how lucky we were. I hoped the extreme nervousness and persistent anxiety and frequent loneliness would likewise disappear, so that I could enjoy completely all the interests I was developing. I didn't understand the complexities and difficulties of growing up, that the people who made up my world were far more varied in their personalities than I yet realised, that frequent failure was an inescapable part of life. By the age of eleven, I was beginning to understand some of this. The age of innocence was over.

The Seeds of Poetry

Raymond Vettese

'Shanks' pony?'

No answer, again.

'I came by Shanks' pony?'

Miss Hodge was a tall thin woman with cropped grey hair. She dressed plainly, in white blouse, grey cardigan, tweed skirt, brown brogues. There was no adornment to offset the austereness. Once a week she taught us Religious Instruction (which consisted mainly of memorizing the books of the Bible), and sometimes English. What has fixed her image in my mind for thirty five years is not so much that mysterious phrase (although I can hear her voice plaint it even yet), but the silence of the Primary Seven class and the brief, pained look on her pallid face as she appealed for one of us to redeem the silence of ignorance. In the end she had to explain that she had walked to work.

A simple enough moment, but it was then, perhaps, that something entered me, struck down its roots.

Or perhaps, it was as early as Primary Two at the Little Academy. The November dusk gathered in the room and the teacher played the piano and we sang, and our piping voices and the happy music among the shadows combined to greatly sadden me, although I did not know why.

Or perhaps it came as I was running home from the Christmas party, running through the frost-bright dark and feeling so full of joy.

Something about light, dark, joy, sorrow, transience, and the eternal glittering of the stars above me.

★

Montrose is an old town, a Royal burgh. At its heart is the steeple, erected in the 1830s. It is a thrust of religious confidence, a leap of faith into the air, an air so often tanged with brine and loud with the kekkle of gulls. It was once a thriving port and the evidence can be seen in some fine housing and on the sea-graves of the Auld Kirkyaird.

In the square in front of the Town Buildings (the Auld Kirk and the steeple are behind this), we gathered to celebrate Hogmanay, to wait for the bell at midnight. We drank from any proffered bottle and kissed any girl willing to be kissed. People still gather there but I haven't been for a long time. I'm told it's not what it was – but then, it never is.

Ten years ago I wrote a poem about that gathering. It begins:

At Hogmanay the steeple clap
dunts oot as tho wi God's muckle nieve
time gane, and wi that dowie chap
lauchin fowk gaithert i the Auld Kirk Square
faa still and micht yet soberly grieve
this ae laist gowp o the deein year,
nane kennin this 'oor whit skelp bides at han'
but thinkin on't whiles, or aiblins coorsely drinkin
so's no til spier ava, fearin there's nocht ower the lan'
save winter cloods an' coontless wanless voices
deavin nae repone as dancer truth gaes glegly jinkin
up an' clean awa intil fremmit places…

In the ensuing verses we go first footing 'or the bottle's duin/ and the sun glowers achingly reid/ on anither horizon.'

The final verses try to bring together the experience of Hogmanay, our knowing of our mortality and our need for something that once, at least, the ceremonies of such as the Auld Kirk provided. Ultimately, it is about achieving wholeness, attaining what Jung called individuation.

Whit we hae seen, been thro, we canna say;
the mindin o't's tapselteerie.
We stotter hame in the cauld licht o Ne'er Day
haen boozed ower deep
and syne tae bed or we wauken yet weary
f'ae a lang drukken sleep
that's no sleep ava but a tyauve wi rest
for sic as us wha speir aye o creation
yet lo'e life wi sic michty zest

and canna settle atween hichts o passion
and howes o despair, kennin nae station,
lookin whiles wi envy on beasts ayont oor confusion

yet kennin tae we canna be as them,
as the tod or the houlet, the ratton or the moose,
steekit i their nicht, wha neither love nor condemn
but simply live, and dee withoot thocht
o resurrection or failure. We canna bide sae crouse
but aye maun pursue whit we aye hae socht,
that vision o perfection, yon crystal dancer
birlin i the sunlicht, brilliantly complete,
ayont time an' duress, needin nae answer
sin answer an' question here are as ane
and aa life's gaithert aneath the whirl o his feet
till a diamond-point death maun shadda in vain!

Wholeness. To be the crystal dancer (the title of the poem), the image of the dancer deriving a little from Yeats, a little from Bob Dylan's 'Tambourine Man' who danced beneath the diamond sky, and from the glittering December streets of Montrose. Light, dark, joy, sorrow, transience and the eternal: the common abiding counters of so much verse.

I became a fan of Bob Dylan's when I was fifteen. I had read somewhere that he'd changed his name from Zimmerman to Dylan in deference to the talent of the Welsh poet. I had little interest in poetry, preferring physics and chemistry as subjects. However, I assumed that this Thomas character would write in the same style and about the same things as my hero and I decided to track his work down at the library (thank you, Andrew Carnegie). I found his *Collected Poems*, took them home, went upstairs to my bedroom and began to read. If there was a moment when that vague 'something', that invisible root, suddenly burst into vivid greeness, it was then. Within five minutes I had been transformed and a long journey was about to begin. I was no longer in my swirling mind the awkward adolescent: I had entered another kingdom, a place once hidden to me and only hinted at in those previous glimpses, if glimpses they were. I had no need of compass, for everything was as familiar to me as the topography of Montrose.

Within weeks I had reams of Thomas's poetry off by heart. I understood implicitly what he was talking about, even in his most obscure passages. Now I began to visit bookshoops to find whatever I could of Dylan's work (I was on first name terms with him by then) and spent my nights reading him: stories, essays, *Under Milkwood, Adventures In The Skin Trade*. I was possessed by his writing, I exulted in his language. The sadness of Miss Hodge I now understood: to be confronted by pupils who were not only ignorant but did not care that they were ignorant. What else was there but words? I loved the very shapes of them and the spaces they filled:

The auld men I speak til
tell me o a life
lang gane, wi horse an' bothy;
nor wad I hae it back,
for weel I ken there's nocht romantic in't.

My ae regret is words,
words rarely heard
on the tongues o newer generations.
But me, I hoard thae words like gowd,
vein them thro verses,
yet no withoot doot,
no withooten the thocht
I'm back in yon times,
wi horse an' bothy,
in a warl best left ahent.

Words arena horses, nor auld men
hirplin, hoastin, tuimm o virr.
Gin I caa, see them rin!
Lowp frae the shroud no deid ava
but bairns, bricht-faced, immortal,
wi aa the secrets o life in their hauns!

I rarely read Dylan Thomas now and I can no longer explain his poetry with the casual assurance born from absolute identification. But those months filled me with a love of poetry that abides. They also filled me with the desire to be a poet. I longed then, at fifteen, to be a great poet. Now I'd settle for being considered a good, albeit minor, one.

★

I was a message boy for Bob Mackenzie, a grocer in North Street. I pedalled his elderly, creaking bicycle through the streets of Montrose and even across the bridge that spans the South Esk to deliver to Rossie Island and the community beyond, Ferryden.

One Saturday in June (a few weeks after discovering Dylan), Montrose changed – or I did. As I pushed the pedals down it was as if I had suddenly cycled into an alternative town, a place existing parallel to Montrose and yet fundamentally different. This town, this Montrose, was charged with gold, streamed with light. Everything glowed. Even the douce grey concrete lamp-posts were surrounded by radiance. And people were enveloped by that same radiance. I knew that I also shone and I felt a mighty surge of love and compassion for all that I saw. And what I saw had slowed down. People inched along the street. My limbs pedalled in fractions. In Christie's Lane I understood everything. I knew absolutely, yet without any words of explanation, the whole purpose. I knew the joy and sorrow of things, the littleness and hugeness of our briefness and immortality. I said aloud OF COURSE! As if this had just been waiting to be found and I had been absurdly stupid not to recognise it before.

I can't really explain that moment in plain language, nor can I properly define it or celebrate it. In later reading I discovered that other people had undergone similar experiences and had also gained a sense of the rightness of things above the calamities that so often engulf our species. "To praise in spite of..." in Rilke's translated phrase.

> Winnocks o siller and the lift sae blue!
> Ye micht forgie ocht this antrin day:
> the ill-gated, the gutsie, the hairtless,
> ay, e'en yersel. That sic a day
> shuid brichten the dour stanes o here,

mak it a moment a place o pure licht!
Wha kens whan sicna growthe micht come
f'ae nocht ava, tho barely oor farin?
But yon's a merely human thocht.
Wha'm I tae judge whit fowk are due?
Winnocks o siller and the lift sae blue
and here a moment a place o pure licht.
That's eneuch. Be glaid. Forgie aa folly,
ay, e'en yer ain. The chance comes but rarely.

Such poems as these, in which I have tried to express something of that experience and the others that followed, don't really do justice to the transformation, but I have found I can only speak obliquely of it, and in fragments of verse.

A few days later I cycled into eternity again, but this time my visit was accompanied by language. I had just delivered groceries to Mrs Gunn, an elderly crippled woman of whom I was very fond. She was a trusting soul who left her front door unlocked. I was to put the groceries away in the kitchen (she was upstairs in bed often) and then I was to take a threepenny bit from her purse, which she left on the table. As I rode away from her house in Mount Road I re-entered that other Montrose. Everything was radiant again but this time there was a strange, high-pitched sound in my ears, a sound I would liken to amplified cicadas, and there were words in my head. It was as if I were being spoken to:

Our span, not worth spitting on,
is almost over you
and carries with it
all the cruelties

So it began, the first poem I had ever written. I can't remember the rest of it and have no idea where the jotter is that I wrote it down in. But it carried on, if I recall aright, lamenting the infirmities of old age and ending with a plea that there be more than this.

Two things occur to me now: firstly, the strangeness of my writing poetry at all. I had gone from ignorance of verse to revelling in Dylan to attempting the stuff myself; secondly, it seems I had not truly understood, or was not capable of fathoming and setting down, what the mystery I had lately been involved in meant. Here I was berating life for age, death, and the assorted miseries of existence, when I had seen, felt profoundly, a different existence, one in which benovelence and charity (in its original meaning) was everywhere present. My words and my experiences did not match. I've been trying ever since to make them fit.

The Montrose Academy magazine was due to be produced. Contributions were sought. I entered some poems. Shortly after I was asked by the then head of the English department, Trevor Johns, to visit. He had been impressed by the poems, wanted to know if I had any more. I went home astonished. As my report card shows I was not noted for excellence, academic or otherwise. Suddenly I was being praised. That had never happened to me in school before, except when I won the Progress Prize in Miss Archibald's Primary Three.

I copied out a short poem I had just finished and delivered it to him the next day. There was a touch of bravado about it: another teacher of English had opined that a real poet could make good verse from anything, even a scrapyard. I wanted to be considered 'a real poet' and was provoked. Before I tell more of that, a little detour.

My parents, James and Susan, ran a newsagents in the High Street. We lived above the shop. It was a large house which had once been owned by a photographer. At the top was a very long, high room which let in a great deal of light and, in the summer, heat. We – my brothers Kenneth and Adrian and my sister Frances – called it The Studio, which it had been in the photographer's time. Beside The Studio was The Laboratory, which consisted of three inter-connected rooms. In here, presumably, the pictures had been developed. The last room of the three overlooked the High Street. Standing at the window there one directly faced the steeple at the other end.

Around the time I discovered poetry I also discovered females, and in the way of stricken adolescents I would go up to that room and look out, hoping to see the goddess I yearned for at any given time. As I watched the busyness below I became intrigued by what was, in a sense, a spectacle, with people moving about their own affairs, intent on their own purposes, caught in the act of being alive. I had a feeling of both detachment and engagement. My eyes caught the weather-vane of the steeple. It seemed to gleam very brightly and then I couldn't see anything else but that spire and its glowing peak and then the cicadas came and along with them a new poem. Afterwards, I went downstairs and wrote it in my jotter, the book I can't find. It was addressed to the sun and began:

Sweat-hauler, salt-pusher...

How it continued I have no idea but I know it ended with something like:

And this is surely the Promised Land!

Obviously I was compelled to write poetry, presumably by some subconscious upsurge which certain 'tricks', such as standing still and watching, becoming vacant as it were, facilitated. I read that Tennyson in his younger days was able to induce a trance-like state by repetition of his name and that in this state he could produce poetry. Perhaps I had discovered something similar. Certainly for a year it worked. Not all the time but often enough to produce a number of poems. One of those was my piece of 'bravado', my attempt to prove myself 'a real poet' to a teacher.

To write that, I went up to The Laboratory and stared at the steeple. I though about my first bicycle. I remembered how my father had helped me to learn how to ride it. There was a square of tarmac behind the house and my father ran around holding the bike with me pedalling. Then, without telling, he would let go and for a while, until I realised that he wasn't there and panic's gravity pulled me down, I was master of the machine. I was utterly determined to learn and although I fell off many times I always got up again. Finally I was able to keep my balance and then it was only a matter of practice.

My bicycle was small, as I was, am. It became, of course, more than a bicycle; it became a knight's charger, a cowboy's stallion, and for several years until even I outgrew it, it was my daily 'companion' in games and in races.

I thought of that bicycle, of how it had ended up discarded and sure enough the steeple and the subconscious did the work. I had my proof. The poem was called 'On A Rubbish Dump':

This bike was a horse...

Again, time has abolished the rest and I have no copy, but I know it was about those childhood games. It ended:

The bike has been put to sleep.

Trevor Johns sent this to the *Scotsman* and it was accepted for publication. I was paid two guineas (£2.20). I was rich and famous. What more could a boy of sixteen want?

And then it stopped. No matter how often I stared at the steeple, no matter how often I pedalled my message-bike, no matter how long I walked the streets at night, I could not enter again that other place nor could I hear the cicadas announce their gift. I was abandoned in old Montrose, shut out from the Eden I knew was there. Only once more did something akin happen and then it was almost in mockery, as though I had been judged not fit.

I had taken up playing snooker in the local parlour. One afternoon there was only myself and another, the other happening to be, by common consent, the best snooker player in town. We agreed to play. He broke and I hunched over the cue. And then they came, the cicadas. Maybe I should have made some excuse and left. Maybe I would have written a poem and proved myself worthy again. But I pulled back the cue and – I could play. I could pot the most difficult shot, escape the most difficult snooker. At the end, when I had scored a substantial victory, my opponent dunted the end of his stick on the floor, our morsed etiquette of appreciation. He offered me another game and I was back to normal – useless.

And so it went from me, that vision, or that ability to enter another state. But the desire to be a poet did not leave. For years I would pursue that longing. At that time, though, failing to write poetry I turned to prose, trying to write about a town I called Easthaven (Montrose, naturally) and the people who lived there. I had not the imagination for this, nor had I the talent for narrative. I preferred the concentration of verse and quickly grew bored of having to describe at length. As a result, whatever stories I wrote turned out to be mere anecdotes rather than proper tales and my lifeless efforts only confirmed the sterility that now beset me.

When I was seventeen I left Montrose Academy. I wasn't sorry. Only in the last two years had I made any impression and even with that my Highers were hardly brilliant.

For a month I did little but read. There was no organisation to it: Fielding, Fitzgerald, Faulkner. That idyll could not last. My parents began reminding me that I needed to make a living. The *Montrose Review* was advertising for a reporter. It seemed the kind of job I might be able to do. I was interviewed by the owner, the late William Robertson – an affable man whom I took to immediately – and found myself employed, probably because I had won the paper's literary prize with some of my poems. I was told afterwards that the editor, John Butchart, snorted 'bloody poets' when told I was on the staff.

If I had notions about being the intrepid journalist hotly pursuing a scoop, they were soon eradicated. My mornings consisted mainly of cutting out items from other papers. These were then re-written for publication. My other activities included going around the golf and bowling clubs to note down scores in various competitions. I had to learn to type, of course, and taught myself a two-fingered style on an ancient black Remington that made my desk tremble whenever I stabbed the keys.

John Butchart was an irascible man at time, red-faced, white-haired, scowling-jowled, but he was a good teacher. I also learned from the chief reporter, Sandy Sutherland, who showed me the ropes.

My first attempts must have been pretty dire. I remember getting back the copy and finding it virtually obliterated by red ink. I had to labour at it before it was accepted. Writing for a newspaper was not as easy as I thought it would be. Indeed, it was a craft, but gradually the knack came. I began to understand the importance of a good opening. I started to get in what was deemed vital information (including the age of any woman mentioned) and how to lighten pars. With the almost-obligatory pun, the besetting sin of journalese. As I improved I was allowed to do more: interviewing people, reporting council meetings, reporting on home football matches. I was establishing myself in a small way in the trade.

And I was still trying to write. One of the *Review*'s companion papers, the *Kincardineshire Observer* ('The Squeaker', as it was known locally) published regular short stories. I wrote one and gave it to Mr Robertson. He returned it with the damning comment: 'too glib'. I had become facile! For one who intended to be a serious writer, this was the worst indictment. I began to wonder if journalese was undermining my ambition. Complete nonsense, really, considering I had written nothing of value for several years, but ruffled vanity no doubt takes comfort from delusion. In fact, I was hardly writing or reading at all by them. I was nineteen and most of my nights were spent in the company of Maureen Milne, who worked on the clerical staff.

It was a gift from our veteran columnist, Jack Smith, that changed things. Jack was a marvellous character, full of mischief and fun. He was a gifted raconteur and, as the saying went, could talk all the legs off a donkey. Jack's desk was crammed with photographs and cut-out articles, some of which he used in his column, 'Gable-enders Gossip' (a Gable-endie being the nickname for Montrosians because of the way houses had been built in the town at one time, the gable-end facing out). Jack's memory was prodigious and he was frequently sent old photographs to identify those pictured. Jack had talked about writing a history of Montrose, and was frequently urged to do so, but he died without producing a book that would have made fascinating reading.

Jack's gift was a slender volume of poetry by Hugh MacDiarmid. It had been published in 1948, on rather poor quality paper, but he thought I might find it interesting. As a young reporter, he had known MacDiarmid (Christopher Grieve), who worked for the *Review* and wrote some of his finest poetry whilst living in Montrose.

I knew little of Scottish poetry. At school we had read some of Burns, which I had enjoyed, and Robert Henryson's 'Testament of Cresseid', a marvellous work which I still consider to be one of the finest in our literature. Of MacDiarmid I knew nothing. Indeed, a teacher of English whom I respected had once informed me that his stuff was 'rubbish' and I took his word for it. Jack's book led me to doubt that opinion, although MacDiarmid's verse did not overwhelm me as Dylan Thomas's had done. Still, I found the lyrics memorable, intense yet immense, and they slowly worked in me. I tried 'A Drunk Man Looks at the Thistle' but found it too difficult in parts. Nonetheless, I was aware I was confronting an extraordinary talent, and I began to think about language.

I had rarely used Scots in poetry, except for a few imitations of Burns, and I had never seriously considered using it. To me, it was connected with the past. It was arcane, outmoded. It was the language of my Scottish grandparents, of my parents, of old people. Oh I could speak it when I had to and found it useful when interviewing the elderly, but had not thought it could be, in the twentieth century, a mode of artistic expression. MacDiarmid, and then Garioch, Goodsir Smith and others, changed my outlook. It was a long time, though, before I had the confidence to write in Scots. I was in my mid-twenties before I began composing some rather conventional love lyrics. Those efforts were puny but once I'd gathered a few together I had the temerity to send them off to MacDiarmid. I'd been through the process of soliciting advice from established authors when I was writing bad English poetry, sending my verses to Stewart Conn, poet, playwright and producer for BBC Radio. He was unfailingly kind and I have never forgotten his patience with my persistent doggerel.

MacDiarmid replied with a long, handwritten letter. He praised my poems a little, then went on to reminisce about his days at Montrose. He was off to Canada soon, he added, apologising that he had not written at greater length! I had formed through my reading an image of a cantankerous man. I had been told, by older members of the *Review* staff (Jack excluded), of his faults. Years later I was asked to contribute to a MacDiarmid issue of the literary journal *Chapman*:

That Man Grieve

So there we were, on a windy day at the top of the *Montrose Review* close: Norman, Valda, various dignitaries including ex-provosts, bailies, ministers...

I was thinking of my first days in the editorial department of that elderly weekly paper. I knew little of MacDiarmid's work then, having been educated in Scotland, but I was intrigued when I went into the dingy garret that served as our office to see on the wall a framed hand-written poem. Aha, I thought, a MacDiarmid original! I peered at the manuscript. It was called 'The Links of Montrose' and was signed: Wm.

McGonagall...

I asked some of the senior members of staff if they remembered MacDiarmid. 'That man Grieve', said the punctilious cashier, 'all he left this town was debts'...

'I was given the job, as the youngest reporter, of presenting Grieve with a farewell gift, and as I was making my speech he was very fidgety, kept looking out the window. Eventually I couldn't stand it any more and I said "Chris, why do you keep doing that?" He said: 'I'm trying to get out of here before they come for me, I haven't paid the rent for months...'

So there we were, Norman, Valda, various dignitaries...

'I read some of the poems once. Couldn't make head nor tail of 'em. Rubbish, I thought, all this fake Scots. He didn't speak like that, you know, at least not to me. The Drunk Man? Ay, that just about sums him up.'

'That dreadful man! If he was in the room now, I would walk out!'

So there we were...

I was thinking how, as a young poet, I'd written to him, enclosing some examples of my work. They were feeble efforts and I wasn't sure I'd get a reply, but a week later back came several handwritten pages. After an apology for not writing sooner or at greater length came kindness, advice, philosophy, gossip, and this to a stranger, an incompetent versifier.

The plaque commemorating the poet was unveiled. In the silence that followed the solemn moment somebody laughed...

...an' droont the haill clanjamfrie!...

In 1972 I married Maureen and left the *Review*. The former deed I have never regretted as we approach our silver anniversary; the latter I sometimes consider was a mistake. I had become, as even John Butchart recognised, a good journalist, and I might have gone on to other things. But I was restless, wanted to try something else.

As so often happens, it was a simple thing that directed the change. A young family lived down the *Review* close and their little boy, for some reason, had grown very attached to me. One day, as I walked up the High Street, he came rushing towards me and gave me a hug. My former history teacher, Mrs Dorothy Morrison, happened to pass at this moment. 'Raymond', she said, 'I didn't realise you were so good with children.' Within a few months I had enrolled at Dundee College of Education on a Primary Teaching course. I was given a mature student's grant and in the autumn began on my new career.

I confess I found most of the instruction dull, although that was balanced by the vivacity of the social life, the drinking and the debates that went on in bars such as The Scout.

When I went on my first teaching practice I was aghast. I faced thirty-odd children, or thirty odd children as it seemed to me, and felt a welter of panic. All those eyes staring at me, a long-haired stammering student. How did one control them? What did one say? How exactly did one develop a lesson? The instructions I had yawningly listened to in Methods vanished like snaw frae a dyke. And in the middle of my faltering discourse, as the first stirrings of disobedience rippled through that body, as a wave of perception that this was a target telecommunicated itself from row to row, in walked my assignment tutor. Instantly, and without him saying a word, incipient rebellion quailed. He talked to them for a while and I saw a good teacher in action and I knew how difficult was the task I had placed upon myself. The *Review* looked more attractive by the minute.

I had been sent to a Catholic school, encountering once again the pigeon-holing that my surname had led to. At Montrose Academy I had escaped the vacation services at the Auld Kirk because it was assumed I was of another religion. In fact, I had been reared in St Luke's and St John's Church of Scotland (the building is now, ironically, the office of the *Montrose Review*) but nobody had ever asked or checked.

> The teacher trooped us tae the kirk
> for a service afore the holidays.
> At the door he turns til me an' whispers:
> It's not for the likes of you, Vettese,
> off you go now – an' aff I gaed
> (I hidna the hairt tae disappoint him)

rinnin wi glee intil simmer's freedom.
Gin the mannie thocht me Catholic, weel,
wi sic a surname whit else wad I be?
Oot o syllables he'd biggit a box,
nailed a lid on a kist o assumption.
He wisna the first, winna be laist.

On the matter of my surname, it is often mispronounced. In Italian it should be something like Vay-tay-zay, but in Angus it is pronounced Vi (as in vigour) teezy, and that is the pronunciation I go by, not *Vitesse*, *à la* French, or Vitessy, or any of the other variations I have groaned over.

My three years went quickly and in 1975 I graduated with merit – a surprise to me as I had been lethargic and somewhat dilettante in my appraoch. On Graduation Day I was late as ever and sat in the wrong place. When my name was called I struggled out but I was too far away and my diploma was awarded to me *in absentia*. I made it up to the stage at last, explained in the wings what had happened, and for ages stood there, waiting. At the end, I was announced again. 'Where the hell were you?' whispered the Chancellor as he smilingly handed over the blue cardboard roll. 'I was in the wrong place' I said. 'I might have known' he replied. I'd been up before him on several occasions. Still, I got a big cheer and loud applause. My idiocy had at least been the cause of amusement.

The one thing I was certain of when I left college was that I didn't want to teach. I had a feeling that I was not cut out for it. During my student years I had worked part-time in a pub, The Salutation in Bridge Street, near my home, or rather the attic flat in which Maureen and I lived. It was tiny but we were happy. At that age, what else would we be? I began working in the pub full-time.

If working at the *Review* taught me more about the town and its people, and going to college broadened me in other ways, pulling pints in The Salutation was truly my further education establishment. The owner was an Orcadian, Willie Work, or as the locals said: Will he work? Will he… (fill in the rest yourself). Willie smoked a pipe and took infinite care in stoking it up. It was a ritual: the tobacco carefully crumbled, gently tamped into the bowl; the flame circled until gouts of reek puffed out. Then he would condescend to serve the customers who had had the misfortune to enter at this sacramental moment. It was not a busy place...

From the moment I started behind the bar, I loved it. Willie and I got on famously. I loved his sly humour and his patient ways. Willie never hurried and although the customers joshed him, it was good humoured banter: the overweight, bald, ruddy-faced, thick-bespectacled owner was respected. He was 'his own man' and they knew it and accepted the fact.

An example of his capacity to remain unruffled and to retain order without fuss came at the end of a Saturday night. Two brothers who constantly bickered with each other were the last customers. I began to sweep up. And then the brothers were fighting, rolling on the floor, strangling each other. Willie lit his pipe and came round. He looked down at the squirming bodies. The younger brother was astride the older and he was choking his *frère* in a superannuated instance of sibling rivalry. Willie took a puff and then said: 'Boys, it's closing time.' Instantly, they jumped up, said in unison, 'Right-o, Willie' and went outside to carry on killing each other in the street. Willie went back behind the bar to count the takings.

The Salutation was truly 'a man's pub', where females rarely ventured. It was a spit and sawdust establishment, patronised by fishermen and farmworkers and because we were seldom thrang I had plenty of time to speak to them, to 'crack' about the old days, since most of them were elderly. I learned about the past from them and I re-learned my tongue. Now I knew absolutely that I had to write about them, had to capture something of them, and that I could not do this in any other medium save Scots. I began to try little verse-pictures. On one occasion I was tending bar myself and a big man of the travelling persuasion came in. What follows is exaggerated, for what I hope is comic effect, but is an early attempt at making that place come alive, with a little dig at myself and those who 'nailed a lid on a kist o assumption':

> There wis ae lad wi nieves like neeps;
> Christ he wis coorse, wi slanty een
> that lookit as gin they'd been soused
> in reid ink a fortnicht or mair.
> Gin ye gied him a look:

Whit are ye gawpin at?
Gin ye tried tae lauch it aff:
Whit are ye grinnin at, Buster?
I kent a fecht wis on the cairds
and shair as fate yin o oor lads
wi a drappie ower the score
gets roosed at this hawker bodie,
an' cries him Tink! Hey Tink!
An' quicker nor ye can blink – boof –
the gype gaed heelster-gowdie.
Aa hell broke loose –
glesses fleein, fists, chairs,
and me,
public servant, keeper o the peace,
cooried ahent the bar.
Jees, a tummler whizzed past me lug!
I creepit til the phone an' beggit the bobbies
an' whan they cam the thing broke up,
but nae afore they'd broken up
gey near aa; och, the place wis mair
an infirmary nor a pub.
Whit a nicht! Fower bashit nebs,
a trouch o bluid,
as monie skailt teet as wad mak
twa peanies. The bobbies, acoorse,
lifted the tink.
He turns at the door, hauchers, cries:
Awa ye teuchters! Awa tae hell!
I near aboot gied him a skelp mysel.
Teuchters!

I had turned away from my conventional love-lyrics and had begun to confront the Montrose I knew. The rauchness, the coorseness and the virr of those men in The Salutation entered my writing – and all to the good, I think. I had believed that only in stories could I set down the people of my town and thus begin to understand it and make it available to others, but now I was seized with a determination to do that in verse, to let my version of Montrose kythe in poetry in Scots.

It was not easy at first. I had buried the language for so long that my first attempts were either too light in Scots or too clogged with gleanings from the dictionary. I had to let it breathe, make it sound natural. But I persevered. I recalled how my parents had gone to Italy. My grandfather Guiseppe had banned the speaking of Italian amongst his younger offspring; only the oldest, my Aunt Mary, (being permitted to act as translator) was allowed to be bilingual. He was determined that the family should integrate (hence my being sent to the kirk) and he felt that it was proper to adopt the leid of Brechin. Thus my father grew up to speak broad Scots. Anyway, he was in Italy and for the first few days was as linguistically-challenged as any non-native ignorant tourist. Then, words and phrases began to well up. Lying there in his mind was that forbidden speech which obviously had entered unbidden and lingered. So it was with me in Scots. As I laboured at widening my vocabulary, words and phrases started to return. I could hear my parents, my Scottish grandparents, the men in The Salutation, and I could hear my own voice beginning to grow. I sent some of my new poems to the magazine *Akros*, which ceased to publish a few years ago, and the editor, Duncan Glen, published them. This time, I was utterly sure: I was on my way, and although I did not hear the cicadas I was confident that I was, after all, able to write. I was a poet.

In 1977 The Salutation was under new management and I decided to leave. The hours had become onerous and I once again felt I needed a change. I had also worked at the local cannery owned by Cadbury–Schweppes (but always ‘Chivers’ to Montrosians, after the company that had long owned it) and I returned to it as a full-time employee, on the processing side.

The job suited me perfectly because I could put on ear-muffs, build my pallets (and I am still proud of the pallets I built – they were plumb-true) and think about my poetry. I had begun a poem about my Italian grandfather. This had started in English. I had never known him – he died when I was too young to remember him – therefore I had to create him. I imagined him lonely, looking back to the land he left. The images would not come alive. I decided to try it in Scots and then I found it vivified, and yet not exactly what I had intended. It became a poem about my father, a poem about a cripple, a poem about resurrection. It is strange sometimes how the business modifies. My father is not crippled but still very vigorous at 80, playing golf and his drums daily (almost all of the family play some instrument). Somehow hippit Mrs Gunn had returned, albeit with a change of gender. I had the poem nearly complete when Duncan Glen wrote asking for five pieces. I had four and this, which I called 'A Window Life'. I thought I might get away with sending him it, although I suspected it was incomplete. I typed up the four and began to type up 'Window'. And then Dylan Thomas made his last bow. I remembered a line of his in which he praised the love that 'breaks all rocks'. That line came into my head and formed the basis of the final verse. It is the poem I think in which I let him and MacDiarmid and all the others go and found, after years of striving, my own voice:

My faither's wearied, a window-life
scunners him wha could never thole
hauf-deid fowk wi kirkyaird sowls.
'We're men,' he'd cry, 'no stanes!'

He glowers oot, grumphie, crabbit wi age,
girns at life whar aince he praised
and praises death, speaks o't kindly.
'Tween him an' the warl's mair nor gless;
he's crippelt noo, will never rise.

Gin I could I wad gie my limbs,
I'd gie my hairt, my thrill o bluid.

Ae thing I swear: I'll dicht frae sicht
this crookit thrawn coorse auld man,
he's no my faither.
I'll hae yon man who strode the days
wi sic a virr and purpose it seemed
the very stour o his wake wad bleeze
like gunpooder fuse.

(Hae I no the richt? Whit's truth,
as him o the weak an' reekin hauns
spiert or he turnt awa?)
I'll howk and I'll howk or I yark frae death
an image o diamond tae cut on time
his green-sowled cry: 'We're men, no stanes!'

Untether his life and let it blaw free
throu aa the twisted veins or it play
the bonniest tunes, nae winter's groans
but sangs o spring that move aa rocks!

★

After a year and a half on the factory floor I moved again, to the US. Base at RAF Edzell. I was employed as a clerical officer working in the library at the school, which had at that time about 120 American children.

It was intriguing to discover the differences between the Scottish and American school systems, to witness first-hand holidays such as Thanksgiving. I also had to learn to spell differently and to overcome linguistic difficulties: they couldn't understand me and I had problems with at least some of the accents. I settled down, though, and found myself in a happy environment, dealing with children ranging from Kindergarten (Primary One equivalent) to 8th Grade (Second Year Secondary).

The Americans were keen to know about Scotland and I found myself going back to the history books to increase my knowledge of my country. That interest also seemed to intensify my desire, already great, to write solely in Scots. I felt, too, that I could look on my country with a different perspective, from a distance, as it were, as if abroad.

In 1980 I enrolled with the Open University and after five years hard labour I was immensely proud of the First Class BA degree I obtained. Only two people in Scotland got an Honours First that year. My vanity was irked that I wasn't the only one!

Having that degree enabled me to teach in the American system and I now found myself with a new title: Host Nation teacher educating American children in all things Scottish. I had found a niche. From being one who didn't want to teach I found myself loving the job. I uncovered in myself an ability to tell stories, to make history vivid, and I've been doing it ever since and, without false modesty, I think I'm very good at it.

In 1985 I not only graduated, I also began to write verse at a high rate. Poem after poem went into my notebook to be revised and revised until I thought I had it right. Maureen and I had moved to a larger house in the same close in Bridge Street and I had a book-lined study upstairs. Here, every night, I worked, and almost every night a poem came, sometimes more than one. There were no cicadas but there was no need to stare at the steeple; somehow, whenever I picked up my pen (I always write in longhand first, then type up for revision) words would flow out. And the words were about Montrose and Scotland.

That year, I had been published in a collection, *Four Scottish Poets*. Joy Hendry, the editor of *Chapman*, had been a little critical of my selection but singled out a rather defeatist poem about the current state of Scotland. She was correct in her criticism: I had not given the collection much thought. She was also correct to single out that poem. It was a good one, but it made me think that my attitude was, in Mr Robertson's phrase, 'too glib'. It was, if you like, a facile reaction. It was easy to condemn, easy to write gloomy verse about a decaying country (sad lines are always easier to pen); it was not so easy to be more constructive, to suggest what might be done. I was, and still am, a Scottish nationalist. I had been secretary for Montrose branch and secretary for the now defunct constituency, North Angus and Mearns. I had trudged the streets with leaflets, I had argued on doorsteps, I had been involved in General Election campaigns. My answer, therefore, was obvious: independence. But I knew that many people did not think that way. My father had brought us up to argue. Maureen, when she was first introduced to our family, could not believe the noise we made as we debated. It was, I suppose, an Italian clamour. We abused each other, shouted each other down, fought our corner with passion, and took turns at playing Devil's Advocate. Whatever the topic – religion, ethics, politics – we pounded the fist in favour of our stance. We were all quite capable of enthrallingly defending a position we did not believe in.

The idea for my first collection began to grow: I would write poems about independence, about Scots, and I would write poems against independence, I would cast doubt on the use of Scots. In the process, Montrose featured more and more as a symbol, a place both alive and dead. The opening of 'The Horn, Yirdit' is an example:

> Midnicht and the clock's knap
> jows the slaw 'oor;
> ilka note's a stane's drap
> intil the smoor.
> The toon's deid still, road and street
> tuim. Wha listens on the bell,
> wha cares? 'A quiet retreat'
> Montrose, as douce (bar the smell
> o the Basin's glaur i the sun's glower)
> as the Sunday Post granda nodded ower.

It's a poem about a moribund place, a corrupt language, and the sixth verse concludes:

> The clock knaps the 'oor again, chaps ane.
> Hoo lang's the nicht. Nocht happens here.
> The waves o the sea maun search ilka grain
> in time. In time Montrose micht disappear
> aff the face o the map. Wha kens?
> And be nae mair, gin that, nor the mindin
> o ancients. Wha cares? Nocht biggit o men's
> immortal. The tide's aye grindin
> and the roots o the sea's ettle gang deep
> and silence maun coor us, and we sleep.

To balance that dreichness there were vivacious poems, humorous poems, as wide a range as my talent could encompass. As the material flowed, I found the manuscript growing unwieldy. I had 123 verses and I was beginning to lose sight of my project. I visited Trevor Johns and he helped me to clarify (the book is dedicated to him and my parents) and emend. Each night I was up until two or three in the morning, arranging, re-arranging, trying to get the balance right, to get a sense of oblique narrative into the collection. I played Sibelius' *5th Symphony* endlessly;

there seemed to me to be a clue in that great piece. Finally, after weeks of drudgery, I had honed things down to 47 poems. Still, I sensed, it was incomplete. I visited Trevor again. We talked – and drank – until the wee hours. I staggered a bit on the way home and decided, against Maureen's advice, to have one more crack at it. As I opened my notebook I turned back the clock – the cicadas howled and the poem I needed, 'Tak Pooer!', arrived. It stands virtually as it was written that boozy night, 59 lines long, and at the end that crystal dancer, my image of wholeness, lowps again:

> Celebrate the dancer, brilliantly complete, whase feet
> turn on a focus, whase body gaithers licht
> as it birls, swirls roon' sae fast it near stauns still
> on a diamond-point at the centre o gowden time!

I parcelled up the volume and sent it to Macdonalds of Loanhead, the first publisher whose name I came upon in a booklet. I soon received a letter of acceptance – and a request for more poems. Another 27 were added in a second section. I regretted that because I had wanted *The Richt Noise*, as I had entitled the 48, to stand alone. I had also begun to work on another collection in which these poems would play a part. Now I was virtually cleaned out and I had to start again amassing verse.

The Richt Noise and Ither Poems was a critical success. It won the Saltire Society's Best First Book award, which I received in Edinburgh. It seemed that the long hours had paid off, but I found myself exhausted. For two years I wrote virtually nothing and began to wonder if I had anything more to say. Those verses I did write were not good. They were peelie-wallie efforts, wan imitations of my previous poems.

In 1989 I applied for the William Soutar Fellowship. Soutar's house in Perth had been renovated by the District Council and a writer-in-residence was being sought. I knew Soutar's poetry and I knew about his life: he had spent many years confined to bed by a crippling spinal complaint. I was given the appointment and Maureen and I moved to Perth. The school gave me a year's sabbatical.

Living in Soutar's beautiful house, built by his father John, a master carpenter, I found my writing began to revive. The renovations were still going on when we moved in and for weeks we lived with the painters and decorators who were putting on the final touches. An official opening was then held. Guests crammed into Willie's former bedroom and various speeches were given. As the last guest left the glass lampshade in the ceiling shattered into dozens of dangerous shards, scattered fragments over every chair. That, said David Stevens afterwards, was Willie's ghost, but then Willie would have been a benign ghost and wouldn't have done anyone any harm. Mr Stevens, a retired minister who had once lived in Perth and had known Willie, gave me much information about him. He told me, for instance, that the sycamore at the bottom of the garden had been planted by Willie. When he put down the telephone (he was calling from Glenesk, where he now lives) I immediately wrote this:

At the end o the green a sycamore
spreids muckle brainches; I canna dismiss
ae thocht as I lounge in heat o simmer,
glaid o shade: Willie Soutar planted this.

Aince it wisna tree ava, juist a skelf,
a skrimpit thing, but noo it's undaunted
an' hauds tae heiven the strength o its years,
the sycamore Willie Soutar planted.

Willie's awa, Willie's lang laid doon,
but the seeds in the wind gaed blawin free
and rooted themsels, thrust deep in the land.
Whanever birds sing, it's on Willie's tree.

My year in Perth went too quickly: I would have liked another so that I could further help to forward Willie's reputation as a writer, but by September 1990 I was back in school and Maureen had returned to her job at Sunnyside Royal Hospital. The year had been fruitful for poetry. I had become interested in the Italian side of my identity and wrote several poems about this:

"– a generation seeded in twa earths
that gies us mebbe the richt mix o strengths:
a gless o warm South laced wi North ice."

I had also thought a great deal about Montrose and wrote about the town. I was in my 40s and I was looking back. Even Bob Mackenzie turned up in 'Shrunkelt'. I was returning to my beginnings:

There were cobbles then in George Street
whan I wis young, message-laddie
til Bob Mackenzie, the grocer, North Street.

The bike dunted ower them shook
aa – my banes, my teeth; I thocht thir
(dozent fancy) the shrunkelt skulls

o monie deid. Thoosans o skulls
I forced my wheels ower!
And the craw o youth as I thrust

pedals doon wi the micht o fifteen years,
drave my wheels, my pooer, ower the deid,
whisslin the glaidness o the life I'd got.

No like them, the egg-heided powkers-up
frae the past, the lang-forgotten.
I thrust doon the pedals and thocht me lowsed

o the past, the deid. Ay weel, the cobbles
are gane, alang wi yon whisslin laddie
and Bob Mackenzie, the grocer, North Street.

Macdonalds had ceased publishing and their contracts had been sold to the Saltire Society. They agreed to publish the book and assigned me an editor, George Bruce, the poet. We were glad to be allowed to meet at Willie's house and there tighten the manuscript. It came out as *A Keen New Air* in 1995 and as far as I can tell barely received a critical mention. *Sic transit* ...

It's not a bad collection and has some fine poems in it, but it does not have the force of *The Richt Noise*. Yet once again I find myself unable to write new verse and can only wait and hope. I am still working at the school, but that will come to an end in 1997 when the American base at Edzell closes. And then, who knows?

It seems proper to conclude with a poem, something that is both about Montrose and its central symbol, the steeple, and about language, that obsession I cycled into so many years ago. I still long to hear the cicadas again and still hope that one day I may see again that other Montrose, that Eden whose gates have been closed to me for 30 years but of whose existence I have no doubt. I may yet, in Christie's Lane, understand everything again, utter again that astounded OF COURSE! and it may be that I will at last be ready to form that vision into language.

Dour-hunched in a drizzle
o dreich November
or smoort in haar
frae the bitter North Sea
this toon's forlane.

Yet I've seen
yon steeple-vane
skyre abuin
as gin unfleggit o ocht it wad craw
braisant on aa!

In dourest season
o near-tint sun
that crouseness vaunts
oot o shaddas,
oot o snell-wun narra wynds,

an' ayont, intil nicht,
whar hirsty fields
streetch cauld
yet hause in dairk
the starry maucht o seed.

In dowf season,
dowie, deid still,
abuin frozen breath,
I hear it:
the vieve cry nae death-grupp thraws.

Biographies of Contributors

David Kerr Cameron

I was born on March 24, 1928, on my maternal grandfather's croft, a place of seven sour acres midway between Tarves and Oldmeldrum. My parents were cottars and my early childhood was spent 'flitting' between one farmtoun and the next in the Tarves/Oldmeldrum/Udny area. I went, initially, to Tarves school (enduring the unremitting rabbit dinners provided courtesy of Haddo's keepers' guns), then to Pitmedden school. Despite my much respected dominies' desire that I 'should be a reporter', I left school at fourteen, and my first employment was as the fairly youthful 'second man' on a milk lorry collecting churns through the night from the silent farmtouns and ferrying the milk into still sleeping Aberdeen to a main depot at Leadside Road and, as day dawned, to little dairy shops round the city. Before my fifteenth birthday I went to work in a 'factory' preparing Army motor cycles for D-Day and later served an apprenticeship as a tractor engineer, interrupted by National Service in the RAF. Back in civvy street, I went round the farms of the North East as the firm's mobile repair man. This was in the Fifties when mechanisation was just beginning to really change farming and in the evenings I started writing articles on the subject which began to appear regularly in the *Press and Journal*, the *Banffshire Journal*, *Farming News* and the *Scottish Farmer*. Believing my old dominie might have been right after all, I became in my early twenties Editor/reporter of the *Kirriemuir Herald*, moving later to the *P & J*. After three years with the paper, and now married, I packed a roomy old Wolsley with our (few) belongings and came to London, working first for a farm mechanization magazine but soon returning to newspapers, at first in the East End but then in Fleet Street with the Mirror Group, next as managing editor of *Farming Express*, and eventually with the *Daily Telegraph*, from which I retired after twenty seven years and on which, as its Chief Features Sub-editor, I was closely involved in the printing revolution from hot metal to the new technology. I still work for the paper, doing stand-in shifts and occasional pieces, including book reviews, but now, long-settled on the fringe of Epping Forest, I am again find the time for more serious writing.

Publications:
T*he Ballad and the Plough*; *Willie Gavin, Crofter Man*; *The Cornkister Days*; *A Kist of Sorrows*.

Iain F W K Davidson

Iain Davidson grew up in Aberdeen, attending Queen's Cross Primary School and Robert Gordon's College. After degrees in history and education at Aberdeen University, and teacher training at Aberdeen Training College, he spent over thirty-five years in the field of education, as teacher, educational psychologist, and researcher. Early work in Scotland was followed by lengthy periods abroad, in England and Canada, which made him conscious of exile. He returned to Aberdeen in 1991, and is currently a research fellow in the Department of Education, University of Aberdeen. He hopes that his contribution to *Roots in a Northern Landscape* is only the first of several works dealing with aspects of North East culture.

David Hay

Born in Aberdeen in 1935 he attended Rhynie village school and the Grammar School in Aberdeen. After a period at boarding school in England, about which he writes in his contribution, he graduated from the Natural History Department in Marischal College, the University of Aberdeen in 1958. After post graduate research in the field of fish physiology at Nottingham University he had a period of grammar school teaching. Early in his career, through his friendship with Sir Alister Hardy, former Professor of Zoology at Oxford University, David Hay became interested in religion as a biological phenomenon. Over the past twenty years, for part of that time as Director of the Alister Hardy Research Centre in Oxford, he has been researching into the frequency of report, nature and function of religious and spiritual experience in British and American populations.

He has published numerous academic papers on the subject and in 1995 was awarded a Templeton Prize for an essay published in the *International Journal for the Psychology of Religion* on the current status of Hardy's hypothesis. David Hay's books include *Exploring Inner Space*; *Scientists and Religious Experience*; and *Religious Experience Today: Studying the Facts*. He is in the process of writing two further books on the spirituality of children and adults who have no formal connection with religious institutions.

Currently, David Hay is on the staff of Nottingham University where he works in the Centre for the Study of Human Relations.

STUART HOOD

Born in Edzell, Angus, in 1915. Educated Montrose Academy and Edinburgh University. Graduated in English Literature. Taught briefly. War service included period as POW in Italy and with the Italian partisans. Joined BBC European Services. Ended up as Editor, Television News and then Controller of Programmes, BBC Television. Worked briefly as executive in commercial television. Became freelance writer and producer of television plays and documentaries. Appointed Professor of Film and Television, Royal College of Art. Resigned. Lectured on Media Studies at Goldsmiths College and the University of Sussex, was for several years visiting Fellow at Sussex University.

Stuart Hood has written widely on the media and media sociology. Fiction includes the following novels: *The Circle and the Minotaur*; *In and Out of the Windows*; *A Storm from Paradise* (Saltire Prize); *The Upper Hand*; *The Brutal Heart*; *A Den Of Foxes*; and *The Book of Judith*.

He has translated widely from Italian: Pasolini, Dario Ro, Vincenzo Consolo, Dino Celati and Aldo Busi. Also from French and German (in particular the poems of Erich Fried) and Russian.

CATHIE IMLAH

I was born in Aberdeen in 1928. Educated at schools in Cults and Aberdeen followed by Craibshone College of Agriculture. After having married and raised a family whilst living in Alford, Newmachar and later Oldmeldrum I spent many happy years working for the Department of Agriculture in Aberdeen before retiring in 1990.

Publication

A History of Newmachar

W GORDON LAWRENCE

I was born in Turiff in January, 1934. My parents moved to Aberdeen when I was about three years old and we lived in a small tenement, now demolished, just beside the bridge across the Dee on the road that leads to Stonehaven and the world beyond. When War broke out I was sent to stay with my grandparents and went to King Edward school. This was a near idyllic time in my childhood and adolescence about which I write in my contribution. Later, when I was about eight years old, I went to Ferryhill School. Our year was the first to sit the newfangled 12 plus and out of a class of thirty odd only two, I think, did not go on with a bursary to Gordon's the Grammar, or the High.

School – Robert Gordon's College – I disliked but scraped to university with a bare matriculation. The idea of a university I liked but I was a slack student and I graduated with an ordinary degree. National Service followed with the Gordon Highlanders and then with the Royal Army Educational Corps. I ended my short service commission as a captain. The army was an important moratorium for me.

I then taught for a period before taking a diploma in sociology at Leicester University. I then went to Durham and lectured at Bede College and in the University of Durham. After a sabbatical at Edinburgh University I went to the Tavistock Institute of Human Relations where I stayed for twelve years before going to Shell International. About this time I took my doctorate from Bergische (Wuppertal) University in Germany. Subsequently, I worked in Paris as the President of the International Foundation for Social Innovation. Since 1990 I have been director of IMAGO East West which is an institution for psychodynamic cultural research. I am a teaching Fellow at Lancaster University and recently I was appointed visiting Professor of Organisational Behaviour, the School of Management, Cranfield University.

I have published regularly since 1965, mostly articles, or chapters in books, on the understanding of groups, psychoanalysis in the context of institutions and 'social dreaming' which is a technique of working with dreams which I discovered. Some of these papers have been translated into German, French, Hungarian, Swedish, Bulgarian and Danish.

Publications:
Take a Look; *Exploring Individual and Organisational Boundaries*.

MARION P SWOGGER

I was born in 1936 in Aberdeen; my father was from The Mearns, my mother from Sunningdale, west of London. At the age of four I started attending St Margaret's School for Girls; most of the school had been evacuated to Blackhall Castle, Banchory, and that's where I began an experience I shall be writing about. At the age of seventeen I went up to Aberdeen University, first of all with the intention of studying English, but at the end of the year I changed to History. The History Department actually asked me to do so, a request I'm sure they later regretted, as I didn't actually do much studying at all during my four years. I was far too distracted by the delights of the Mermaid Society, acting with the Dramatic Society, including their first ever appearance at the Edinburgh Festival Fringe Student Show and also editing *Gaudie* the second ever female editor, I believe.

'Real life' burst upon me the following year at London University's Institute of Education when I had to confront a class of teenagers for the first time. It took several despairing months before terror turned into enjoyment.

My first teaching post was at the Chaterlard School in Switzerland, an institution long since defunct, and not surprisingly so. However, it did have some wonderfully eccentric angles; it possessed an exquisite theatre (the building had formerly been a hotel in the 19th century) and Noel Coward used to use it as a rehearsal room!

It soon became obvious to me that I needed to learn my work 'from the bottom up' and this I proceeded to do at the Abbey School, Reading, where as assistant teacher of History, English and Scripture, I often had to learn new material very fast indeed! It was now that I began to study seriously for myself. Stimulated by a lecture on Pylos by our wonderful Classics teacher I began to read widely on classical history and art. Subsequent travels, in particular to Italy, Greece (where I worked for a far too short but unforgettable time) and Romania developed my interest in and knowledge of Byzantine art and history.

At the age of thirty I had already been head of a History Department for three years, and the next obvious step was to become an Assistant Head Mistress. But I had no wish to be an administrator, nor any ability in that direction. I was bored not with the teaching as such, just its limitations in a school environment. Also, I wanted to go back to University and this time really embrace the opportunity to learn, to extend myself intellectually. So I returned to Aberdeen, as a very rusty scholar, to obtain a Diploma in Medieval Studies and, in the course of that year, to discover what did engage my deepest enthusiasm. The answer became clear: learning about art in the historical, cultural, and religious context. The next step was an M. Litt. The subject of my thesis: Post Byzantine Art in Cyprus, with particular reference to the scene of the Holy Women at the Tomb. This was a happy and fortunate combination of all my academic enthusiasms, amongst which is a fascination with the minutiae of doctrinal differences, which interest of mine I still don't understand as I am personally and emotionally totally pragmatic about what I consider as inessential details compared with larger truths.

I had intended to start a new career in the developing field of Museum Education and in fact had already obtained a position, when my life took a completely new direction and I was not to return to this (for me) ideally stimulating and satisfying work until six years ago. Marriage brought with it five changes of country in seven years and three babies. It was through a mixture of preference and lack of possibilities that over the years I became a full-time Mum. For the last 18 years, I've lived in Hanover, New Hampshire, where fortunately over the years there have been endless opportunities for a wide variety of volunteer work, usually involving working with children and teenagers. In addition, I was able to write occasional articles on Orthodox iconography. Also I had ever expanding areas of study to explore: Middle East history and politics, Islam, Islamic Art, Moghul India, the British in India, and through my work with the Hanover Historical Society I did master some American history as well! For the last six years I have worked as a Docent at the Hood Museum at Dartmouth College; we deal with such a variety of exhibits that practically everything I've studied throughout my life has come in useful on my tours and in addition I'm constantly stimulated by new areas of interest, African religion and art in particular. Most of the children I deal with come from low income rural areas and a single 'Wow! That's really interesting! Tell us more!' fulfils all the ambitions I've ever had in my life.

RAYMOND VETTESE

I was born in Arbroath on the 1st of November, 1950, the son of an Italian father and a Scottish mother. In the early 50s the family emigrated to the States but eventually the family returned to Scotland and subsequently moved to Montrose. I have lived in the town for some forty years and think I can pass myself off as a 'Gable ender', despite having elements of the Brechin dialect (both my parents come from that City) in my speech!

I was educated at 'the wee Academy' as it was known, and then Montrose Academy. At the age of fourteen I began to write verse, having come under the influence of Dylan Thomas. At fifteen I had a poem accepted by the *Scotsman* and I thought I was famous! I was not a diligent student, alas, and left school with only three Highers. I got a job as a reporter with the *Montrose Review* and it was there that I first really came into contact with the work of Hugh McDiarmid who had also worked on that newspaper. I had neglected writing for a number of years but his verse stimulated me to try my hand at poetry in Scots with, of course, the Angus dialect predominant. I have written almost solely in Scots since. My work began to be published in magazines and in 1988 my first collection emerged, *The Richt Noise*, which won the Saltire Society's award for Best First Book. In 1995 my second collection, *A Keen New Air*, was published.